H E A T H
MIDDLE LEVEL
LITERATURE

Friends

Whatever we do and wherever we go, there is one thing that we need more than anything else—the friends that share our lives. How would you define friendship?

A U T H O R S

Donna Alvermann
Linda Miller Cleary
Kenneth Donelson
Donald Gallo
Alice Haskins
J. Howard Johnston
John Lounsbury
Alleen Pace Nilsen
Robert Pavlik
Jewell Parker Rhodes
Alberto Alvaro Ríos
Sandra Schurr
Lyndon Searfoss
Julia Thomason
Max Thompson
Carl Zon

D.C. Heath and Company
Lexington, Massachusetts / Toronto, Ontario

STAFF CREDITS

EDITORIAL	Barbara A. Brennan, Helen Byers, Christopher Johnson, Kathleen Kennedy Kelley, Owen Shows, Rita M. Sullivan
	Proofreading: JoAnne B. Sgroi
CONTRIBUTING WRITERS	Nance Davidson, Florence Harris
SERIES DESIGN	Robin Herr
BOOK DESIGN	Caroline Bowden, Daniel Derdula, Susan Geer, Diana Maloney, Angela Sciaraffa, Bonnie Chayes Yousefian
	Art Editing: Carolyn Langley
PHOTOGRAPHY	*Series Photography Coordinator:* Carmen Johnson
	Photo Research Supervisor: Martha Friedman
	Photo Researchers: Wendy Enright, Po-yee McKenna, PhotoSearch, Inc., Gillian Speeth, Denise Theodores
	Assignment Photography Coordinators: Susan Doheny, Gayna Hoffman, Shawna Johnston
COMPUTER PREPRESS	Ricki Pappo, Kathy Meisl, Richard Curran, Michele Locatelli
PERMISSIONS	Dorothy B. McLeod
PRODUCTION	Patrick Connolly

Cover Design: Steve Snider

Acknowledgments for copyrighted material are on page 125 and constitute an extension of this page.

Published simultaneously in Canada

Printed in the United States of America

International Standard Book Number: 0-669-32099-4
1 2 3 4 5 6 7 8 9 10-RRD-99 98 97 96 95 94

Middle Level Authors

Donna Alvermann, University of Georgia
Alice Haskins, Howard County Public Schools, Maryland
J. Howard Johnston, University of South Florida
John Lounsbury, Georgia College
Sandra Schurr, University of South Florida
Julia Thomason, Appalachian State University
Max Thompson, Appalachian State University
Carl Zon, California Assessment Collaborative

Literature and Language Arts Authors

Linda Miller Cleary, University of Minnesota
Kenneth Donelson, Arizona State University
Donald Gallo, Central Connecticut State University
Alleen Pace Nilsen, Arizona State University
Robert Pavlik, Cardinal Stritch College, Milwaukee
Jewell Parker Rhodes, California State University, Northridge
Alberto Alvaro Ríos, Arizona State University
Lyndon Searfoss, Arizona State University

Teacher Consultants

Suzanne Aubin, Patapsco Middle School, Ellicott City, Maryland
Judy Baxter, Newport News Public Schools, Newport News, Virginia
Saundra Bryn, Director of Research and Development, El Mirage, Arizona
Lorraine Gerhart, Elmbrook Middle School, Elm Grove, Wisconsin
Kathy Tuchman Glass, Burlingame Intermediate School, Burlingame, California
Lisa Mandelbaum, Crocker Middle School, Hillsborough, California
Lucretia Pannozzo, John Jay Middle School, Katonah, New York
Carol Schultz, Jerling Junior High, Orland Park, Illinois
Jeanne Siebenman, Grand Canyon University, Phoenix, Arizona
Gail Thompson, Garey High School, Pomona, California
Rufus Thompson, Grace Yokley School, Ontario, California
Tom Tufts, Conniston Middle School, West Palm Beach, Florida
Edna Turner, Harpers Choice Middle School, Columbia, Maryland
C. Anne Webb, Buerkle Junior High School, St. Louis, Missouri
Geri Yaccino, Thompson Junior High School, St. Charles, Illinois

CONTENTS

THE LITERATURE

Midtown Sunset Romare Bearden, Private collection

ASKING BIG QUESTIONS ABOUT THE LITERATURE

PROJECTS

1 WRITING WORKSHOP

A FRIENDSHIP MEMOIR 106-111

Capture your memories of a special friend.

2 COOPERATIVE LEARNING

ADVERTISING A FRIENDSHIP WEEK 112-113

Develop an advertising campaign for a week of activities focusing on friendship.

3 HELPING YOUR COMMUNITY

A FRIEND-TO-MY-COMMUNITY DAY 114-115

Practice a different kind of friendship by making your community a better place to live.

INVENT-A-FRIE

Develop 1 your theory.

Scientists begin their experiments with a theory or unproven idea. First, they decide what the task is; then they think of ways to accomplish it. Think about what your perfect or ideal friend would be like. What character traits are important to you—appearance, age, special abilities? On a sheet of paper, develop your theory by brainstorming a list of character traits to complete this sentence: An ideal friend is someone who _____.

Collect 2 and evaluate your data.

Because they know that not all data is useful, scientists try to weed out details that weaken their theories. Once you've brainstormed a list of character traits, evaluate them and decide which ones you want to keep. To help you select the most important traits, discuss situations in which a special personality trait or physical characteristic would be a positive feature to have. For example, if you are shy, a friend who is outgoing may make social events less awkward for you.

Think of it! You're a scientist puttering in your laboratory—but your laboratory is a writing laboratory. It's your task to invent an ideal friend by using a mixture of words. What words will you choose, and how will you combine them? To test your ideas about friendship, complete the following steps individually, in a small group, or with your whole class.

3 Organize your data.

Scientists have to present their data well to get others to understand and support them. To organize your data, create a chart or poster. Write your theory at the top. Under the theory, write the traits you've selected from your list. Be sure you can provide specific examples and reasons to support your choices.

4 Test your conclusions.

If scientists didn't evaluate their results, they'd have no idea if their theories would work. Test your conclusions by comparing and contrasting the character traits of your ideal friend with the ones selected by other students. What are the similarities and differences? What new perspective did you get on the ideal friend?

Asking Big Questions About the Theme

What does it mean to be a friend?

In your journal, write a recipe for how to be a friend. List the ingredients and their measurements first, followed by instructions for combining them. Then compare your recipe with those of your classmates.

What does it mean to have a friend?

In your journal, create a web like the one started here. At the center of the web, write the name of someone, either real or imaginary, that you think would be a good friend. Then fill in the web with nouns, verbs, adjectives, and adverbs describing the friend's importance in your life. Share the web with a partner.

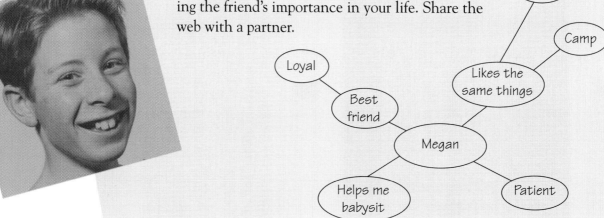

What are different kinds of friendship?

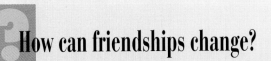

In your journal, draw several concentric circles like the ones shown and label them with the places you spend time, such as neighborhood, school, and camp. Then write the names of friends within the appropriate circles. Some friends' names may appear in more than one circle. Discuss with a partner the similarities and differences among these friendships.

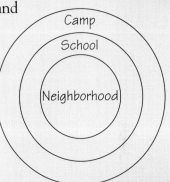

Camp

School

Neighborhood

How can friendships change?

What events in your life have caused changes in your friendships? In your journal, create a time line like the one shown to trace the progress of your friendships. Divide the line into the different periods of your life and place important events in their appropriate position. Share your time line with several classmates and explain why these particular events are important to you.

NOW

Think!

Suppose that you have to explain friendship to someone who has never experienced it. With a partner, brainstorm ways to explain it and record your ideas in your journal. Then, as you read the literature in this unit, compare your ideas about friendship with the types of friendships experienced by the characters in the selections. Does your explanation of friendship change?

Billy and I go to Camp.	Join Little League	Best friends with Kyle	Started Junior High
8 yrs. old	10 yrs. old	11 yrs. old	12 yrs. old

THE BRACELET

Evacuee Family and Baggage   Minè Okubo, 1943, gouache on paper, 15¹/₂" x 19¹/₂"

Yoshiko Uchida

"The Bracelet"
Yoshiko Uchida

"**M**ama, is it time to go?"

I hadn't planned to cry, but the tears came suddenly, and I wiped them away with the back of my hand. I didn't want my older sister to see me crying.

"It's almost time, Ruri," my mother said gently. Her face was filled with a kind of sadness I had never seen before.

I looked around at my empty room. The clothes that Mama always told me to hang up in the closet, the junk piled on my dresser, the old rag doll I could never bear to part with; they were all gone. There was nothing left in my room, and there was nothing left in the rest of the house. The rugs and furniture were gone, the pictures and drapes were down, and the closets and cupboards were empty. The house was like a gift box after the nice thing inside was gone; just a lot of nothingness.

It was almost time to leave our home, but we weren't moving to a nicer house or to a new town. It was April 21, 1942. The United States and Japan were at war, and every Japanese person on the West Coast was being evacuated[1] by the government to a concentration camp.[2] Mama, my sister Keiko[3] and I were being sent from our home, and out of Berkeley, and eventually, out of California.

The doorbell rang, and I ran to answer it before my sister could. I thought maybe by some miracle, a messenger from the government might be standing there, tall and proper and buttoned into a uniform, come to tell us it was all a terrible mistake; that we wouldn't have to leave after all. Or maybe the messenger would have a telegram from Papa, who was interned in a prisoner-of-war camp in Montana because he had worked for a Japanese business firm.

1. **evacuated** [i vak′ yü āt əd]: forced to leave.
2. **concentration camp** [kon′ sən trā′ shən]: in this case, a relocation camp; one of several inland detention camps established by the United States government during World War II for all Japanese Americans living on the West Coast.
3. **Keiko** [kā′ kō]

The FBI had come to pick up Papa and hundreds of other Japanese community leaders on the very day that Japanese planes had bombed Pearl Harbor.[4] The government thought they were dangerous enemy aliens.[5] If it weren't so sad, it would have been funny. Papa could no more be dangerous than the mayor of our city, and he was every bit as loyal to the United States. He had lived here since 1917.

When I opened the door, it wasn't a messenger from anywhere. It was my best friend, Laurie Madison, from next door. She was holding a package wrapped up like a birthday present, but she wasn't wearing her party dress, and her face drooped like a wilted tulip.

"Hi," she said. "I came to say goodbye."

She thrust the present at me and told me it was something to take to camp. "It's a bracelet," she said before I could open the package. "Put it on so you won't have to pack it." She knew I didn't have one inch of space left in my suitcase. We had been instructed to take only what we could carry into camp, and Mama had told us that we could each take only two suitcases.

"Then how are we ever going to pack the dishes and blankets and sheets they've told us to bring with us?" Keiko worried.

"I don't really know," Mama said, and she simply began packing those big impossible things into an enormous duffel bag—along with umbrellas, boots, a kettle, hot plate, and flashlight.

"Who's going to carry that huge sack?" I asked.

But Mama didn't worry about things like that. "Someone will help us," she said. "Don't worry." So I didn't.

Laurie wanted me to open her package and put on the bracelet before she left. It was a thin gold chain with a heart dangling on it. She helped me put it on, and I told her I'd never take it off, ever.

"Well, good-bye then," Laurie said awkwardly. "Come home soon."

"I will," I said, although I didn't know if I would ever get back to Berkeley again.

4. **Pearl Harbor:** United States naval base in Hawaii, which Japan attacked on December 7, 1941, bringing the United States into World War II.
5. **aliens** [ā′ lyənz]: people who are not citizens of the country in which they live.

I watched Laurie go down the block, her long blond pigtails bouncing as she walked. I wondered who would be sitting in my desk at Lincoln Junior High now that I was gone. Laurie kept turning and waving, even walking backwards for a while, until she got to the corner. I didn't want to watch anymore, and I slammed the door shut.

The next time the doorbell rang, it was Mrs. Simpson, our other neighbor. She was going to drive us to the Congregational church, which was the Civil Control Station where all the Japanese of Berkeley were supposed to report.

It was time to go. "Come on, Ruri. Get your things," my sister called to me.

It was a warm day, but I put on a sweater and my coat so I wouldn't have to carry them, and I picked up my two suitcases. Each

Drawing by detention camp internee Minè Okubo

one had a tag with my name and our family number on it. Every Japanese family had to register and get a number. We were Family Number 13453.

Mama was taking one last look around our house. She was going from room to room, as though she were trying to take a mental picture of the house she had lived in for fifteen years, so she would never forget it.

I saw her take a long last look at the garden that Papa loved. The irises beside the fish pond were just beginning to bloom. If Papa had

been home, he would have cut the first iris blossom and brought it inside to Mama. "This one is for you," he would have said. And Mama would have smiled and said, "Thank you, Papa San,"[6] and put it in her favorite cut-glass vase.

But the garden looked shabby and forsaken now that Papa was gone and Mama was too busy to take care of it. It looked the way I felt, sort of empty and lonely and abandoned.

Drawing by detention camp internee Minè Okubo

When Mrs. Simpson took us to the Civil Control Station, I felt even worse. I was scared, and for a minute I thought I was going to lose my breakfast right in front of everybody. There must have been over a thousand Japanese people gathered at the church. Some were old and some were young. Some were talking and laughing, and some were crying. I guess everybody else was scared too. No one knew exactly what was going to happen to us. We just knew we were being taken to the Tanforan Racetracks, which the army had turned into a camp for the Japanese. There were fourteen other camps like ours along the West Coast.

What scared me most were the soldiers standing at the doorway of the church hall. They were carrying guns with mounted bayonets. I wondered if they thought we would try to run away, and whether they'd shoot us or come after us with their bayonets if we did.

6. **San** [sän]: term of respect added to Japanese names.

A long line of buses waited to take us to camp. There were trucks, too, for our baggage. And Mama was right; some men were there to help us load our duffel bag. When it was time to board the buses, I sat with Keiko and Mama sat behind us. The bus went down Grove Street and passed the small Japanese food store where Mama used to order her bean-curd cakes and pickled radish. The windows were all boarded up, but there was a sign still hanging on the door that read, "We are loyal Americans."

The crazy thing about the whole evacuation was that we were all loyal Americans. Most of us were citizens because we had been born here. But our parents, who had come from Japan, couldn't become citizens because there was a law that prevented any Asian from becoming a citizen. Now everybody with a Japanese face was being shipped off to concentration camps.

Drawing by detention camp internee Minè Okubo

"It's stupid," Keiko muttered as we saw the racetrack looming up beside the highway. "If there were any Japanese spies around, they'd have gone back to Japan long ago."

"I'll say," I agreed. My sister was in high school and she ought to know, I thought.

When the bus turned into Tanforan, there were more armed guards at the gate, and I saw barbed wire strung around the entire grounds. I felt as though I were going into a prison, but I hadn't done anything wrong.

We streamed off the buses and poured into a huge room, where doctors looked down our throats and peeled back our eyelids to see if we had any diseases. Then we were given our housing assignments. The man in charge gave Mama a slip of paper. We were in Barrack[7] 16, Apartment 40.

"Mama!" I said. "We're going to live in an apartment!" The only apartment I had ever seen was the one my piano teacher lived in. It was in an enormous building in San Francisco with an elevator and thick carpeted hallways. I thought how wonderful it would be to have our own elevator. A house was all right, but an apartment seemed elegant and special.

We walked down the racetrack looking for Barrack 16. Mr. Noma, a friend of Papa's, helped us carry our bags. I was so busy looking around, I slipped and almost fell on the muddy track. Army barracks had been built everywhere, all around the racetrack and even in the center oval.

Mr. Noma pointed beyond the track toward the horse stables. "I think your barrack is out there."

He was right. We came to a long stable that had once housed the horses of Tanforan, and we climbed up the wide ramp. Each stall had a number painted on it, and when we got to 40, Mr. Noma pushed open the door.

"Well, here it is," he said. "Apartment 40."

The stall was narrow and empty and dark. There were two small windows on each side of the door. Three folded army cots were on the dust-covered floor and one light bulb dangled from the ceiling. That was all. This was our apartment, and it still smelled of horses.

Mama looked at my sister and then at me. "It won't be so bad when we fix it up," she began. "I'll ask Mr. Simpson to send me some material for curtains. I could make some cushions too, and . . . well . . . ." She stopped. She couldn't think of anything more to say.

Mr. Noma said he'd go get some mattresses for us. "I'd better hurry before they're all gone." He rushed off. I think he wanted to leave so that he wouldn't have to see Mama cry. But he needn't have

7. **barrack** [barʹ ək]: a large building in which soldiers usually live.

run off, because Mama didn't cry. She just went out to borrow a broom and began sweeping out the dust and dirt. "Will you girls set up the cots?" she asked.

It was only after we'd put up the last cot that I noticed my bracelet was gone. "I've lost Laurie's bracelet!" I screamed. "My bracelet's gone!"

We looked all over the stall and even down the ramp. I wanted to run back down the track and go over every inch of ground we'd walked on, but it was getting dark and Mama wouldn't let me.

I thought of what I'd promised Laurie. I wasn't ever going to take the bracelet off, not even when I went to take a shower. And now I had lost it on my very first day in camp. I wanted to cry.

I kept looking for it all the time we were in Tanforan. I didn't stop looking until the day we were sent to another camp, called Topaz, in the middle of a desert in Utah. And then I gave up.

But Mama told me never mind. She said I didn't need a bracelet to remember Laurie, just as I didn't need anything to remember Papa or our home in Berkeley or all the people and things we loved and had left behind.

"Those are things we can carry in our hearts and take with us no matter where we are sent," she said.

And I guess she was right. I've never forgotten Laurie, even now.

YOSHIKO UCHIDA

Yoshiko Uchida [1921-1992] was born in Alameda, California. The Uchida family members' lives changed terribly during World War II, when the government interned all Japanese Americans in concentration camps. Suddenly the Uchidas became Family Number 13453 and were taken first to one and then to another prison camp. The camps were so crowded, Uchida said, that people had "no place to cry and no place to hide."

Uchida said the story of the Japanese American internments, "as painful as it may be to hear, needs to be told and retold and never forgotten." You can read more about her family's experience in her books *Journey to Topaz* and *Journey Home*.

A bald display solidarity

ASSOCI

...ATED PRESS

YORKVILLE, Ill.—Treatment for leukemia[1] soon may cost Mark Lowry his hair, but his bald head won't stand out in the classrooms at Cross Lutheran School.

When the school's 15 other seventh- and eighth-grade boys learned that Mark, 13, would undergo the chemotherapy,[2] they decided to have their own heads shaved in a show of support.

By Thursday, only two of the 16 weren't bald. One, Robert Erickson, was waiting for the weekend for his clipping. The other was Mark ... ho came home Wednesday from the hospital with a full head of h...

...n't be for long though," he said. "And my dad ...ok like the rest of the guys."

...learned only recently that he had ...v treatments last week.

...rless?

...unanimous[3] response.

in the

Form 21

ADMISSION SLIP

EXCUSED

Date_____

has made explanation of the {TARDINESS / ABSENCE} listed below:

Remarks:_____

Re-Admitted to Classes.

Date___ 3/19

Period_____

Teacher_____

School Service Co., Inc., Grayslake, Illinois 60030

OUR GOOD DAY

SANDRA CISNEROS

If you give me five dollars I will be your friend forever. That's what the little one tells me.

Five dollars is cheap since I don't have any friends except Cathy who is only my friend till Tuesday.

Five dollars, five dollars.

She is trying to get somebody to chip in so they can buy a bicycle from this kid named Tito. They already have ten dollars and all they need is five more.

Electric Prisms Sonia Delaunay, 1914, National Museum of Modern Art, Paris, France

Only five dollars, she says.

Don't talk to them, says Cathy. Can't you see they smell like a broom.

But I like them. Their clothes are crooked and old. They are wearing shiny Sunday shoes without socks. It makes their bald ankles all red, but I like them. Especially the big one who laughs with all her teeth. I like her even though she lets the little one do all the talking.

Five dollars, the little one says, only five.

Cathy is tugging my arm and I know whatever I do next will make her mad forever.

Wait a minute, I say, and run inside to get the five dollars. I have three dollars saved and I take two of Nenny's. She's not home, but I'm sure she'll be glad when she finds out we won a bike. When I get back, Cathy is gone like I knew she would be, but I don't care. I have two new friends and a bike too.

My name is Lucy, the big one says. This here is Rachel my sister.

I'm her sister, says Rachel. Who are you?

And I wish my name was Cassandra or Alexis or Maritza— anything but Esperanza—but when I tell them my name they don't laugh.

We come from Texas, Lucy says and grins. Her was born here, but me I'm Texas.

You mean *she*, I say.

No, I'm from Texas, and doesn't get it.

This bike is three ways ours, says Rachel who is thinking ahead already. Mine today, Lucy's tomorrow and yours day after.

But everybody wants to ride it today because the bike is new, so we decide to take turns *after* tomorrow. Today it belongs to all of us.

I don't tell them about Nenny just yet. It's too complicated. Especially since Rachel almost put out Lucy's eye about who was going to get to ride it first. But finally we agree to ride it together. Why not?

Because Lucy has long legs she pedals. I sit on the back seat and Rachel is skinny enough to get up on the handlebars which makes the bike all wobbly as if the wheels are spaghetti, but after a bit you get used to it.

We ride fast and faster. Past my house, sad and red and crumbly in places, past Mr. Benny's grocery on the corner, and down the avenue which is dangerous. Laundromat, junk store, drug store, windows and cars and more cars, and around the block back to Mango.

People on the bus wave. A very fat lady crossing the street says, You sure got quite a load there.

Rachel shouts, You got quite a load there too. She is very sassy.

Down, down Mango Street we go. Rachel, Lucy, me. Our new bicycle. Laughing the crooked ride back.

SANDRA CISNEROS

Sandra Cisneros was born in Chicago in 1954 and grew up there, in a neighborhood like the one in "Our Good Day." Later she moved to San Antonio, Texas. When she isn't teaching, she writes what she calls the "kind of stories I didn't get growing up. Stories about poor families, brown families. People I knew and loved, but never saw in the pages of the books I borrowed from the Chicago Public Library."

Cisneros writes both prose and poetry. She says, "Fiction is a way to change the community, right wrongs, wail about grievances, fight back, push, shove, shake, terrorize. Poems are more like howls of the heart." "Our Good Day" is from her book of short stories, *The House on Mango Street*.

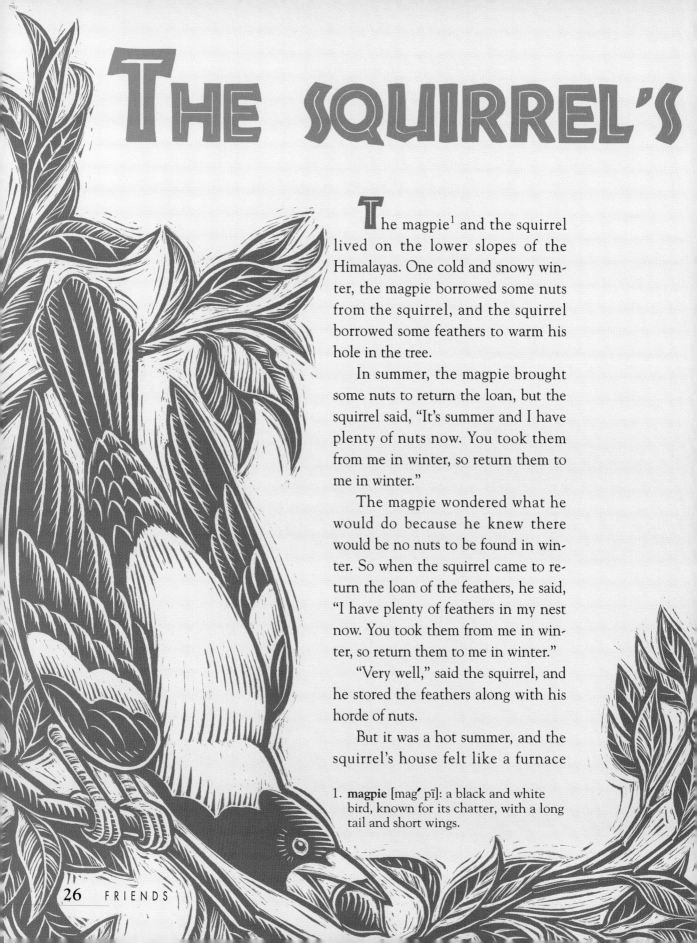

THE SQUIRREL'S

The magpie[1] and the squirrel lived on the lower slopes of the Himalayas. One cold and snowy winter, the magpie borrowed some nuts from the squirrel, and the squirrel borrowed some feathers to warm his hole in the tree.

In summer, the magpie brought some nuts to return the loan, but the squirrel said, "It's summer and I have plenty of nuts now. You took them from me in winter, so return them to me in winter."

The magpie wondered what he would do because he knew there would be no nuts to be found in winter. So when the squirrel came to return the loan of the feathers, he said, "I have plenty of feathers in my nest now. You took them from me in winter, so return them to me in winter."

"Very well," said the squirrel, and he stored the feathers along with his horde of nuts.

But it was a hot summer, and the squirrel's house felt like a furnace

1. **magpie** [mag′ pī]: a black and white bird, known for its chatter, with a long tail and short wings.

LOAN

Partap Sharma

with all those feathers in it. So he threw the feathers out, thinking he'd pick them up when winter came around and it was time to return the loan.

In winter, there was ice and snow everywhere. The feathers were buried underneath. Try as he might, the squirrel could not dig them out.

He said to the magpie, "I'm afraid I can't find feathers in winter."

"Nor can I find nuts at this time," said the magpie.

And the squirrel remembered his loan and his words to the magpie, and he was ashamed. He said, "I should expect you to return the nuts when you can, not when you cannot. A loan is meant to help a friend, not to give him trouble."

From then on they helped each other in winter and repaid their debts in summer. They continued to live happily and became even better friends thereafter.

Ring, Ring Roy Lichtenstein, 1961, oil on canvas, 24" x 16"

TELEPHONE TALK

X. J. KENNEDY

Back flat on the carpet,
Cushion under my head,
Sock feet on the wallpaper,
Munching raisin bread,

Making easy whispers   5
Balance on high wire,
Trading jokes and laughing,
The two of us conspire, [1]

Closer than when walking
Down the street together,   10
Closer than two sparrows
Hiding from wet weather.

How would my shrill whistle
Sound to you, I wonder?
Give a blow in *your* phone,   15
My phone makes it thunder.

Through the night, invisibly
Jumping over space,
Back and forth between us
All our secrets race.   20

1. **conspire** [kən spīr′]: plan secretly
   together.

X. J. KENNEDY

X. J. Kennedy was born in 1929 in Dover, New Jersey. After graduating from Seton Hall University and serving in the Navy during the Korean War, he became an English professor and writer of textbooks. Later he began to write poetry and prose for both adults and young people.

Kennedy enjoys writing poems that make use of traditional patterns of rhyme and meter. He thinks composing this kind of poetry can be both challenging and fun, "an enormous, meaningful game" that includes interesting discoveries for the poet.

Besides *The Kite That Braved Old Orchard Beach*, you can look up collections of Kennedy's humorous verse for young people, including *The Phantom Ice Cream Man*, *The Forgetful Wishing Well*, and *Brats*.

A Time To Talk

ROBERT FROST

When a friend calls to me from the road
And slows his horse to a meaning[1] walk,
I don't stand still and look around
On all the hills I haven't hoed,
And shout from where I am, "What is it?"   5
No, not as there is a time to talk.
I thrust my hoe in the mellow ground,
Blade-end up and five feet tall,
And plod:[2] I go up to the stone wall
For a friendly visit.   10

1. meaning: expressive, significant.
2. plod: walk heavily or slowly.

ROBERT FROST

Robert Frost [1874-1963] was born in San Francisco but later moved to Lawrence, Massachusetts. After high school he worked as a bobbin boy in a textiles mill, a cobbler, a newspaper editor, a teacher, and a farmer—but always dreamed of making poetry his career.

Frost moved to England in 1912, where he published two books of poems about rural New England. In 1915, he returned to America and became known as New England's poet and one of the great American poets. You can find Frost's poems in many collections, including *You Come Too: Favorite Poems for Young Readers*.

Wood engraving
Thomas W. Nason,
Boston Public Library
Print Department

The Osage Orange

WILLIAM STAFFORD

On that first day of high school in the prairie town where the tree was, I stood in the sun by the flagpole and watched, but pretended not to watch, the others. They stood in groups and talked and knew each other, all except one—a girl though—in a faded blue dress, carrying a sack lunch and standing near the corner looking everywhere but at the crowd.

I might talk to her, I thought. But of course it was out of the question.

That first day was easier when the classes started. Some of the teachers were kind; some were frightening. Some of the students didn't care, but I listened and waited; and at the end of the day I was relieved, less conspicuous from then on.

But that day was not really over. As I hurried to carry my new paper route, I was thinking about how in a strange town, if you are quiet, no one notices, and some may like you, later. I was thinking about this when I reached the north edge of town where the scattering houses dwindle. Beyond them to the north lay just openness, the plains, a big swoop of nothing. There, at the last house, just as I cut across a lot and threw to the last customer, I saw the girl in the blue dress coming along the street, heading on out of town, carrying books. And she saw me.

"Hello."

"Hello."

And because we stopped we were friends. I didn't know how I could stop, but I didn't hurry on. There was nothing to do but to act

Tree

as if I were walking on out too. I had three papers left in the bag, and I frantically began to fold them—box them, as we called it—for throwing. We had begun to walk and talk. The girl was timid; I became more bold. Not much, but a little.

"Have you gone to school here before?" I asked.

"Yes, I went here last year."

A long pause. A meadowlark sitting on a fencepost hunched his wings and flew. I kicked through the dust of the road.

I began to look ahead. Where could we possibly be walking to? I couldn't be walking just because I wanted to be with her.

Fortunately, there was one more house, a gray house by a sagging barn, set two hundred yards from the road.

"I thought I'd see if I could get a customer here," I said, waving toward the house.

"That's where I live."

"Oh."

We were at the dusty car tracks that turned off the road to the house. The girl stopped. There was a tree at that corner, a straight but little tree with slim branches and shiny dark leaves.

"I could take a paper tonight to see if my father wants to buy it."

A great relief, this. What could I have said to her parents? I held out a paper, dropped it, picked it up, brushing off the dust. "No, here's a new one"—a great action, putting the dusty paper in the bag over my shoulder and pulling out a fresh one. When she took the paper we stood there a minute. The wind was coming in over the grass. She looked out with a tranquil[1] expression.

She walked away past the tree, and I hurried quickly back toward town. Could anyone in the houses have been watching? I looked back once. The girl was standing on the small bridge halfway into her house. I hurried on.

The next day at school I didn't ask her whether her father wanted to take the paper. When the others were there I wouldn't say anything. I stood with the boys. In American history the students could choose their seats, and I saw that she was too quiet and plainly dressed for many to notice her. But I crowded in with the boys, pushing one aside, scrambling for a seat by the window.

That night I came to the edge of town. Two papers were left, and I walked on out. The meadowlark was there. By some reeds in a ditch by the road a dragonfly—snake feeders, we called them—glinted. The sun was going down, and the plains were stretched out and lifted, some way, to the horizon. Could I go on up to the house? I didn't think so, but I walked on. Then, by the tree where her road turned off, she was standing. She was holding her books. More confused than ever, I stopped.

"My father will take the paper," she said.

She told me always to leave the paper at the foot of the tree. She insisted on that, saying their house was too far; and it is true that I was far off my route, a long way, a half-mile out of my territory. But I didn't think of that.

And so we were acquainted. What I remember best in that town is those evening walks to the tree. Every night—or almost every night—the girl was there. Evangeline was her name. We didn't say much. On Friday night of the first week she gave me a dime, the cost

1. **tranquil** [trang′kwəl]: calm, peaceful.

of the paper. It was a poor newspaper, by the way, cheap, sensational,[2] unreliable. I never went up to her house. We never talked together at school. But all the time we knew each other; we just happened to meet. Every evening.

There was a low place in the meadow by that corner. The fall rains made a pond there, and in the evenings sometimes ducks would be coming in—a long line with set wings down the wind, and then a turn, and a skimming glide to the water. The wind would be blowing and the grass bent down. The evenings got colder and colder. The wind was cold. As winter came on the time at the tree was dimmer, but not dark. In the winter there was snow. The pond was frozen over; all the plains were white. I had to walk down the ruts of the road and leave the paper in the crotch of the tree, sometimes, when it was cold. The wind made a sound through the black branches. But usually, even on cold evenings, Evangeline was there.

At school we played ball at noon—the boys did. And I got acquainted. I learned that Evangeline's brother was janitor at the school. A big dark boy he was—a man, middle-aged I thought at the time. He didn't ever let on that he knew me. I would see him sweeping the halls, bent down, slow. I would see him and Evangeline take their sack lunches over to the south side of the building. Once I slipped away from the ball game and went over there, but he looked at me so steadily, without moving, that I pretended to be looking for a book, and quickly went back, and got in the game and struck out.

You don't know about those winters, and especially that winter. Those were the dust years.[3] Wheat was away down in price. Everyone was poor—poor in a way that you can't understand. I made two dollars a week, or something like that, on my paper route. I could tell about working for ten cents an hour—and then not getting paid; about families that ate wheat, boiled, for their main food, and burned wheat for fuel. You don't know how it would be. All through that

2. **sensational** [sen sā′ shə nəl]: trying to arouse strong feelings.
3. **dust years:** the Great Depression in the 1930s, when the American Midwest and Southwest suffered droughts and destructive dust storms.

hard winter I carried a paper to the tree by the pond, in the evening, and gave it to Evangeline.

In the cold weather Evangeline wore a heavier dress, a dark, straight, heavy dress, under a thick black coat. Outdoors she wore a knitted cap that fastened under her chin. She was dressed this way when we met and she took the paper. The reeds were broken now. The meadowlark was gone.

And then came the spring. I have forgotten to tell just how Evangeline looked. She was of medium height, and slim. Her face was pale, her forehead high, her eyes blue. Her tranquil face I remember well. I remember her watching the wind come in over the grass. Her dress was long, her feet small. I can remember her by the tree, with her books, or walking on up the road toward her house and stopping on the bridge halfway up there, but she didn't wave, and I couldn't tell whether she was watching me or not. I always looked back as I went over the rise toward town.

And I can remember her in the room at school. She came into American history one spring day, the first really warm day. She had changed from the dark heavy dress to the dull blue one of the last fall; and she had on a new belt, a gray belt, with blue stitching along the edges. As she passed in front of Jane Wright, a girl who sat on the front row, I heard Jane say to the girl beside her, "Why look at Evangeline—that old dress of hers has a new belt!"

"Stop a minute, Evangeline," Jane said; "let me see your new dress."

Evangeline stopped and looked uncertainly at Jane and blushed. "It's just made over," she said, "it's just . . . "

"It's cute, Dear," Jane said; and as Evangeline went on Jane nudged her friend in the ribs and the friend smothered a giggle.

Well, that was a good year. Commencement[4] time came, and—along with the newspaper job—I had the task of preparing for finals and all. One thing, I wasn't a student who took part in the class play or anything like that. I was just one of the boys—twenty-fourth in line to get my diploma.

4. **commencement** [kə mens′ ment]: graduation.

And graduation was bringing an end to my paper-carrying. My father covered a big territory in our part of the state, selling farm equipment; and we were going to move at once to a town seventy miles south. Only because of my finishing the school year had we stayed till graduation.

I had taught another boy my route, always leaving him at the end and walking on out, by myself, to the tree. I didn't really have to go around with him that last day, the day of graduation, but I was going anyway.

At the graduation exercises, held that May afternoon, I wore my brown Sunday suit. My mother was in the audience. It was a heavy day. The girls had on new dresses. But I didn't see her.

I suppose that I did deserve old man Sutton's "Shhh!" as we lined up to march across the stage, but I for the first time in the year forgot my caution, and asked Jane where Evangeline was. She shrugged, and I could see for myself that she was not there.

We marched across the stage; our diplomas were ours; our parents filed out; to the strains of a march on the school organ we trailed to the hall. I unbuttoned my brown suit coat, stuffed the diploma in my pocket, and sidled out of the group and upstairs.

Evangeline's brother was emptying wastebaskets at the far end of the hall. I sauntered toward him and stopped. I didn't know what I wanted to say. Unexpectedly, he solved my problem. Stopping his work, holding a partly empty wastebasket over the canvas sack he wore over his shoulder, he stared at me, as if almost to say something.

"I noticed that your sister wasn't here," I said. The noise below was dwindling. The hall was quiet, an echoey place; my voice sounded terribly loud. He emptied the rest of the wastebasket and shifted easily. He was a man, in big overalls. He stared at me.

"Evangeline couldn't come," he said. He stopped, looked at me again, and said, "She stole."

"Stole?" I said. "Stole what?"

He shrugged and went toward the next wastebasket, but I followed him.

"She stole the money from her bank—the money she was to use

for her graduation dress," he said. He walked stolidly[5] on, and I stopped. He deliberately turned away as he picked up the next waste-basket. But he said something else, half to himself. "You knew her. You talked to her . . . I know." He walked away.

I hurried downstairs and outside. The new carrier would have the papers almost delivered by now; so I ran up the street toward the north. I took a paper from him at the end of the street and told him to go back. I didn't pay any more attention to him.

No one was at the tree, and I turned, for the first time, up the road to the house. I walked over the bridge and on up the narrow, rutty tracks. The house was gray and lopsided.[6] The ground of the yard was packed; nothing grew there. By the back door, the door to which the road led, there was a grayish-white place on the ground where the dishwater had been thrown. A gaunt shepherd dog trotted out growling.

And the door opened suddenly, as if someone had been watching me come up the track. A woman came out—a woman stern-faced, with a shawl over her head and a dark lumpy dress on—came out on the back porch and shouted, "Go 'way, go 'way! We don't want no papers!" She waved violently with one hand, holding the other on her shawl, at her throat. She coughed so hard that she leaned over and put her hand against one of the uprights of the porch. Her face was red. She glanced toward the barn and leaned toward me. "Go 'way!"

Behind me a meadowlark sang. Over all the plains swooped the sky. The land was drawn up somehow toward the horizon.

I stood there, half-defiant, half-ashamed. The dog continued to growl and to pace around me, stiff-legged, his tail down. The windows of the house were all blank, with blinds drawn. I couldn't say anything.

I stood a long time and then, lowering the newspaper I had held out, I stood longer, waiting, without thinking of what to do. The

5. **stolidly** [stol′ id lē]: showing no emotion.
6. **lopsided** [lop′ sī′ did]: leaning to one side.

meadowlark bubbled over again, but I turned and walked away, looking back once or twice. The old woman continued to stand, leaning forward, her head out. She glanced at the barn, but didn't call out any more.

My heels dug into the grayish place where the dishwater had been thrown; the dog skulked along behind.

At the bridge, halfway to the road, I stopped and looked back. The dog was lying down again; the porch was empty; and the door was closed. Turning the other way, I looked toward town. Near me stood our ragged little tree—an Osage orange tree it was. It was feebly coming into leaf, green all over the branches, among the sharp thorns. I hadn't wondered before how it grew there, all alone, in the plains country, neglected. Over our pond some ducks came slicing in.

Standing there on the bridge, still holding the folded-boxed-newspaper, that worthless paper, I could see everything. I look out along the road to town. From the bridge you would see the road going away, to where it went over the rise.

Glancing around, I flipped that last newpaper under the bridge and then bent far over and looked where it had gone. There they were—a pile of boxed newspapers, thrown in a heap, some new, some worn and weathered, by rain, by snow.

WILLIAM STAFFORD

....

William Stafford was born in Kansas in 1914 and raised on a farm there. Stafford's college career was interrupted during World War II when he served as as a conscientious objector in civilian public service camps and relief organizations.

Stafford has taught at colleges in the Midwest and in Oregon. His fame as a writer comes from his poetry, although he is well known for stories such as "The Osage Orange Tree."

One poem of Stafford's that is especially well known is "Fifteen." You can find it in his book *The Rescued Year*. Other Stafford books include *West of Your City* and *Traveling Through the Dark*.

Where Are Now, William Shakes

My very first boyfriend was named William Shakespeare. This was his real name, and he lived over on Highland Hill, about a block from my house.

Billy Shakespeare didn't call at seven for dates, or suffer my father's inspection, or give me a silver identification bracelet. We didn't have a song, either.

I often went to his house to get him, or I met him down in the empty lot on Alden Avenue, or over at Hoopes Park, where we caught sunfish and brought them from the pond in bottles of murky water with polliwogs.

Marijane is ten [my father wrote in his journal]. *She plays with boys and looks like one.*

This was true.

My arms and knees were full of scabs from falls out of trees and off my bicycle. I was happiest wearing the pants my brother'd grown out of, the vest to one of my father's business suits over one of my brother's old shirts, Indian moccasins, and a cap. Everything I said came out of the side of my mouth, and I strolled around with my fists inside my trouser pockets.

you peare?

M. E. KERR

This did not faze Billy Shakespeare, whose eyes lit up when he saw me coming, and who readily agreed that when we married we'd name our first son Ellis, after my father, and not William after him.

"Because William Shakespeare is a funny name," I'd say.

"It isn't funny. It's just that there's a famous writer with the same name," he'd say.

"Do you agree to Ellis Shakespeare then?"

"Sure, if it's all right with your father."

"He'll be pleased," I'd tell Billy.

Around this time, I was always trying to think of ways to please my father. (The simplest way would have been to wear a dress and a big hair ribbon, stay out of trees, stop talking out of the side of my mouth, and act like a girl . . . but I couldn't have endured such misery even for him.)

Billy Shakespeare accepted the fact, early in our relationship, that my father was my hero. He protested only slightly when I insisted that the reason my father wasn't President of the United States was that my father didn't want to be.

That was what my father told me, when I'd ask him why he wasn't President. I'd look at him across the table at dinner, and think, He knows more than anybody knows, he's handsome, and he always gets things done—so he ought to be President. If he was, I'd think, there'd be no problems in the world.

Sometimes I'd ask him: "Daddy, why aren't you President of the United States?"

His answer was always the same.

"I wouldn't want that job for anything. We couldn't take a walk without Secret Service[1] men following us. Do you think we could go up to the lake for a swim by ourselves? No. There'd be Secret Service men tagging along. It'd ruin our lives. It'd end our privacy. Would you want that?"

Billy Shakespeare would say, "He's not President because nobody elected him President."

"He won't let anyone elect him," I'd answer. "He doesn't want Secret Service men around all the time."

"I'm not sure he could *get* elected," Billy would venture.

"He could get elected," I'd tell Billy. "He doesn't want to! We like our privacy!"

"Okay." Billy'd give in a little. "But he never tried getting elected, so he really doesn't know if he could."

I'd wave that idea away with my dirty hands. "Don't worry. He'd be elected in a minute if he wanted to be. You don't know *him*."

Billy Shakespeare's other rivals for my attention were movie stars. I'd write Clark Gable and Henry Fonda and Errol Flynn, and they'd send back glossy photos of themselves and sometimes letters, too.

These photographs and letters were thumbtacked to the fiberboard walls of a playhouse my father'd had built for me in our backyard.

When I did play with a girl, the game was always the same: getting dinner ready for our husbands. I had an old set of dishes back in the playhouse, and my girl friend and I played setting the table for dinner. During this game, Billy Shakespeare was forgotten. When my husband came through the playhouse door, he would be one of the movie stars pinned to the wall.

I played this game with Dorothy Spencer, who lived behind our house.

She was a tall redhead who looked like a girl,

1. **Secret Service:** the branch of the United States Department of the Treasury that provides protection for the President and his immediate family.

and who always had it in her head to fix meat loaf with mashed potatoes for a movie star named Spencer Tracy.

I changed around a lot—the menu as well as the movie star—but Dorothy stuck to meat loaf with mashed for Spencer.

I'd be saying, "Well, Clark is a little late tonight and the turkey is going to be overdone," or "Gee, Henry isn't here yet and the ham is going to be dried up." But Dorothy would persist with "Spencer's going to love this meat loaf when he gets here. I'll wait until I hear his footsteps to mash the potatoes."

Billy Shakespeare was jealous of this game and tried his best to ruin it with reality.

He'd say, "What are two famous movie stars doing living in the same house?"

He'd say, "How come famous movie stars only have a one-room house with no kitchen?"

But Dorothy Spencer and I went on happily playing house, until the movie *Brother Rat* came to town.

That was when we both fell in love with the movie star Ronald Reagan.[2]

Suddenly we were both setting the table for the same movie star—different menus, but the same husband.

"You've always stuck to meat loaf and mashed for Spencer!" I said angrily. "Now you want my Ronald!"

"He's not *your* Ronald," she said.

"It's my playhouse, though," I reminded her.

"But I won't play if I can't have Ronald," she said.

"We both can't have Ronald!" I insisted.

We took the argument to her mother, who told us to pretend Ronald Reagan was twins. Then we could both have him.

"He isn't twins, though," Dorothy said.

"And if he is," I put in, "I want the real Ronald, and not his twin."

Our game came to a halt, but our rivalry did not. Both of us had written to Ronald Reagan and were waiting for his reply.

2. **Ronald Reagan:** former movie star who became the fortieth president of the United States.

"No matter what he writes her," I told Billy Shakespeare, "my letter from him will be better."

"You might not even get a letter," Billy said. "She might not get one either."

"She might not get one," I said, "but I will."

"You don't know that," Billy said.

"Do you want to know why I know I'll get one?" I asked him.

I made him cross his heart and hope to die if he told anyone what I'd done.

Billy was a skinny little kid with big eyes that always got bigger when I was about to confess to him something I'd done.

"Crossmyheartandhopetodie," he said very fast. "What'd you do?"

"You know that Ronald Reagan isn't like any of the others," I said.

"Because Dorothy Spencer likes him, too."

"That's got nothing to do with it!" I said. "He's just different. I never felt this way about another movie star."

"Why?"

"*Why?* I don't know why! That's the way love is."

"Love?" Billy said.

"Yes. What did you think made me write him that I was a crippled child, and had to go to see him in a wheelchair?"

"Oh migosh!" Billy exclaimed. "Oh migosh!"

"I had to get his attention somehow."

"Oh migosh!"

"Just shut up about it!" I warned him. "If word gets out I'll know it's you."

Dorothy Spencer was the first to hear from Ronald Reagan. She didn't get a letter, but she got a signed photograph.

"Since I heard from him first," she said, "he's my husband."

"Not in my playhouse!" I said.

"He wrote me back first," she said.

"Just wait," I said.

"I don't have to wait," she said. "I'm setting the table for him in my own house."

"It's not even your house, it's your father's," I said. "At least when he's married to me, we'll have our own house."

"He's married to me now," she said.

"We'll see about that," I said.

I was beginning to get a panicky feeling as time passed and no mail came from Ronald Reagan. You'd think he'd write back to a crippled child first. . . . .Meanwhile Dorothy was fixing him meat loaf and mashed at her place.

I had pictures of him cut out of movie magazines scotch-taped to my bedroom walls. I went to sleep thinking about him, wondering why he didn't care enough to answer me.

The letter and photograph from Ronald Reagan arrived on a Saturday.

I saw the Hollywood postmark and let out a whoop, thereby attracting my father's attention.

"What's all the excitement?"

I was getting the photograph out of the envelope. "I got a picture from Ronald Reagan!"

"Who's he?"

"Some movie star," my mother said.

By that time I had the photograph out. My heart began to beat nervously as I read the inscription at the bottom. "To a brave little girl, in admiration, Ronald Reagan."

"What does it say?" my father said.

"Nothing, it's just signed," I said, but he already saw what it said as he stood behind me looking down at it.

"Why are you a brave little girl?" he asked.

"How do I know?" I said.

"There's a letter on the floor," said my mother.

"That's my letter," I said, grabbing it.

"Why are you considered a brave little girl?" asked my father again. "Why does *he* admire *you*?"

I held the letter to my chest. "Those are just things they say," I said.

"They say you're *brave?*" my father said.

"Brave or honest or any dumb thing," I said weakly.

"Read the letter, Marijane," said my father.

I read the letter to myself.

Dear Marijane,
Thank you for your letter.
Remember that a handicap can be a challenge.
Always stay as cheerful as you are now.
Yours truly,
Ronald Reagan

"What does it say?" my mother asked.

"Just the usual," I said. "They never say much."

"Let me see it, brave little girl," my father said.

"It's to me."

"Marijane . . ." and he had his hand out.

After my father read the letter, and got the truth out of me concerning my correspondence with Ronald Reagan, he told me what I was to do.

What I was to do was to sit down immediately and write Ronald Reagan, telling him I had lied. I was to add that I thanked God for my good health. I was to return both the letter and the photograph.

No Saturday in my entire life had ever been so dark.

My father stood over me while I wrote the letter in tears, convinced that Ronald Reagan would hate me all his life for my deception. I watched through blurred eyes while my father took my letter, Ronald Reagan's letter, and the signed photograph, put them into a manila envelope, addressed it, sealed it, and put it in his briefcase to take to the post office.

For weeks and weeks after that, I dreaded the arrival of our postman. I was convinced a letter'd come beginning,

Dear Marijane,
How very disappointed I am in you. . . .

"I don't think he'll write back," Billy Shakespeare told me. "I don't think he'll want anything more to do with you."

That ended getting dinner for movie stars in my playhouse.

I told Dorothy Spencer that I'd outgrown all that.

Three years after I wrote Ronald Reagan that letter, I slumped way down in my seat in humiliation as I watched him lose a leg in the movie *King's Row.* . . . I was sure he thought of the little liar from upstate New York who'd pretended she was crippled.

Many, many years later, the man I always thought should be President of the United States was dead, and Ronald Reagan was President of the United States.

I didn't vote for him.

I heard Dorothy Spencer got married, and I envision her making meat loaf and mashed for her husband.

The only remaining question is, Where are you now, William Shakespeare?

M. E. KERR

M. E. Kerr was born in 1927 in Auburn, New York. Her real name is Meaker—M. E. Kerr pronounced another way! Like many writers, Kerr has used different "pen names" when writing such different kinds of books as suspense novels and nonfiction. Kerr has said it was after writing her first young adult novel that "things that happened to me long ago came back clear as a bell and ringing." Those memories gave her the ideas she was looking for.

M. E. Kerr has written many books, including *The Son of Someone Famous* and *I'll Love You When You're More Like Me*. The nonfiction story you've just read is a chapter in her autobiography, *Me, Me, Me, Me, Me: Not a Novel*.

"Mom" Sammy Henry Bozeman Jones, 1938, lithograph, 9" x 6 3/4", The Howard University Gallery of Art, Washington, D.C.

Thank You, M'am

LANGSTON HUGHES

She was a large woman with a large purse that had everything in it but hammer and nails. It had a long strap and she carried it slung across her shoulder. It was about eleven o'clock at night, and she was walking alone, when a boy ran up behind her and tried to snatch her purse. The strap broke with the single tug the boy gave it from behind. But the boy's weight and the weight of the purse combined caused him to lose his balance, so instead of taking off full blast as he had hoped, the boy fell on his back on the sidewalk, and his legs flew up. The large woman simply turned around and kicked him right square in his blue-jeaned sitter. Then she reached down, picked the boy up by his shirt front, and shook him until his teeth rattled.

After that the woman said, "Pick up my pocketbook, boy, and give it here."

She still held him. But she bent down enough to permit him to stoop and pick up her purse. Then she said, "Now ain't you ashamed of yourself?"

Firmly gripped by his shirt front, the boy said, "Yes'm."

The woman said, "What did you want to do it for?"

The boy said, "I didn't aim to."

She said, "You a lie!"

By that time two or three people passed, stopped, turned to look, and some stood watching.

"If I turn you loose, will you run?" asked the woman.

"Yes'm," said the boy.

"Then I won't turn you loose," said the woman. She did not release him.

"I'm very sorry, lady, I'm sorry," whispered the boy.

"Um-hum! And your face is dirty. I got a great mind to wash your face for you. Ain't you got nobody home to tell you to wash your face?"

"No'm," said the boy.

"Then it will get washed this evening," said the large woman starting up the street, dragging the frightened boy behind her.

He looked as if he were fourteen or fifteen, frail and willow-wild, in tennis shoes and blue jeans.

The woman said, "You ought to be my son. I would teach you right from wrong. Least I can do right now is to wash your face. Are you hungry?"

"No'm," said the being-dragged boy. "I just want you to turn me loose."

"Was I bothering *you* when I turned that corner?" asked the woman.

"No'm."

"But you put yourself in contact with *me*," said the woman. "If you think that that contact is not going to last awhile, you got another thought coming. When I get through with you, sir, you are going to remember Mrs. Luella Bates Washington Jones."

Sweat popped out on the boy's face and he began to struggle. Mrs. Jones stopped, jerked him around in front of her, put a half nelson[1] about his neck, and continued to drag him up the street. When she got to her door, she dragged the boy inside, down a hall, and into a large kitchenette-furnished room at the rear of the house. She switched on the light and left the door open. The boy could hear other roomers laughing and talking in the large house. Some of their doors were open, too, so he knew he and the woman were not alone. The woman still had him by the neck in the middle of her room.

She said, "What is your name?"

"Roger," answered the boy.

"Then, Roger, you go to that sink and wash your face," said the

1. **half nelson:** in wrestling, a hold applied by hooking one arm under the opponent's armpit and putting a hand on the back of the opponent's neck.

Midtown Sunset Romare Bearden, 1981, collage on board, 14" x 22",
Private collection

woman, whereupon she turned him loose—at last. Roger looked at
the door—looked at the woman—looked at the door—*and went to
the sink.*

"Let the water run until it gets warm," she said. "Here's a
clean towel."

"You gonna take me to jail?" asked the boy, bending over the
sink.

"Not with that face, I would not take you nowhere," said the
woman. "Here I am trying to get home to cook me a bite to eat and
you snatch my pocketbook! Maybe you ain't been to your supper
either, late as it be. Have you?"

"There's nobody home at my house," said the boy.

"Then we'll eat," said the woman. "I believe you're hungry—
or been hungry—to try to snatch my pocketbook!"

"I wanted a pair of blue suede[2] shoes," said the boy.

"Well, you didn't have to snatch *my* pocketbook to get some suede shoes," said Mrs. Luella Bates Washington Jones. "You could of asked me."

"M'am?"

The water dripping from his face, the boy looked at her. There was a long pause. A very long pause. After he had dried his face and not knowing what else to do dried it again, the boy turned around, wondering what next. The door was open. He could make a dash for it down the hall. He could run, run, run, run, *run!*

The woman was sitting on the day-bed. After awhile she said, "I were young once and I wanted things I could not get."

There was another long pause. The boy's mouth opened. Then he frowned, but not knowing he frowned.

The woman said, "Um-hum! You thought I was going to say *but*, didn't you? You thought I was going to say, *but I didn't snatch people's pocketbooks.* Well, I wasn't going to say that." Pause. Silence. "I have done things, too, which I would not tell you, son—neither tell God, if he didn't already know. So you set down while I fix us something to eat. You might run that comb through your hair so you will look presentable."

In another corner of the room behind a screen was a gas plate and an icebox. Mrs. Jones got up and went behind the screen. The woman did not watch the boy to see if he was going to run now, nor did she watch her purse which she left behind her on the day-bed. But the boy took care to sit on the far side of the room where he thought she could easily see him out of the corner of her eye, if she wanted to. He did not trust the woman *not* to trust him. And he did not want to be mistrusted now.

"Do you need somebody to go to the store," asked the boy, "maybe to get some milk or something?"

"Don't believe I do," said the woman, "unless you just want sweet milk yourself. I was going to make cocoa out of this canned milk I got here."

2. **suede** [swād]: a soft leather that feels velvety on one or both sides.

"That will be fine," said the boy.

She heated some lima beans and ham she had in the icebox, made the cocoa, and set the table. The woman did not ask the boy anything about where he lived, or his folks, or anything else that would embarrass him. Instead, as they ate, she told him about her job in a hotel beauty-shop that stayed open late, what the work was like, and how all kinds of women came in and out, blondes, red-heads, and Spanish. Then she cut him a half of her ten-cent cake.

"Eat some more, son," she said.

When they were finished eating she got up and said, "Now, here, take this ten dollars and buy yourself some blue suede shoes. And next time, do not make the mistake of latching onto *my* pocketbook *nor nobody else's*— because shoes come by devilish like that will burn your feet. I got to get my rest now. But I wish you would behave yourself, son, from here on in."

She led him down the hall to the front door and opened it. "Goodnight! Behave yourself, boy!" she said, looking out into the street.

The boy wanted to say something else other than, "Thank you, m'am," to Mrs. Luella Bates Washington Jones, but he couldn't do so as he turned at the barren stoop and looked back at the large woman in the door. He barely managed to say, "Thank you," before she shut the door. And he never saw her again.

LANGSTON HUGHES

Langston Hughes [1902-1967] was born in Joplin, Missouri. During his life, Hughes traveled so widely that he called his autobiography "I Wonder as I Wander." However, no matter how many continents he visited, the subject of his poems and stories continued to be the life he knew best—the daily experience of African Americans. Hughes wrote mainly of city life and everyday people whose strength of character could make a difference.

Fighter with Manager James Weeks, 1960, oil on canvas, 214" x 168", Private collection

AMIGO BROTHERS

PIRI THOMAS

*A*ntonio Cruz and Felix Varga were both seventeen years old. They were so together in friendship that they felt themselves to be brothers. They had known each other since childhood, growing up on the lower east side of Manhattan in the same tenement[1] building on Fifth Street between Avenue A and Avenue B.

Antonio was fair, lean, and lanky, while Felix was dark, short, and husky. Antonio's hair was always falling over his eyes, while Felix wore his black hair in a natural Afro[2] style.

Each youngster had a dream of someday becoming lightweight champion of the world. Every chance they had the boys worked out, sometimes at the Boys Club on 10th Street and Avenue A and sometimes at the pro's gym on 14th Street. Early morning sunrises would find them running along the East River Drive, wrapped in sweat shirts, short towels around their necks, and handkerchiefs Apache style around their foreheads.

While some youngsters were into street negatives, Antonio and Felix slept, ate, rapped, and dreamt positive. Between them, they had a collection of *Fight* magazines second to none, plus a scrapbook filled with torn tickets to every boxing match they had ever attended, and some clippings of their own. If asked a question about any given fighter, they would immediately zip out from their memory banks divisions, weights, records of fights, knockouts, technical knockouts, and draws or losses.

Each had fought many bouts representing their community and had won two gold-plated medals plus a silver and bronze medallion.

---

1. **tenement** [ten′ ə mənt]: an apartment house in a large city.
2. **Afro** [af′ rō]: a full, natural hair style.

The difference was in their style. Antonio's lean form and long reach made him the better boxer, while Felix's short and muscular frame made him the better slugger. Whenever they had met in the ring for sparring sessions, it had always been hot and heavy.

Now, after a series of elimination bouts, they had been informed that they were to meet each other in the division finals that were scheduled for the seventh of August, two weeks away—the winner to represent the Boys Club in the Golden Gloves Championship Tournament.

The two boys continued to run together along the East River Drive. But even when joking with each other, they both sensed a wall rising between them.

One morning less than a week before their bout, they met as usual for their daily workout. They fooled around with a few jabs at the air, slapped skin, and then took off, running lightly along the dirty East River's edge.

Antonio glanced at Felix who kept his eyes purposely straight ahead, pausing from time to time to do some fancy leg work while throwing one-twos followed by upper cuts to an imaginary jaw. Antonio then beat the air with a barrage of body blows and short devastating lefts with an overhand jaw-breaking right.

After a mile or so, Felix puffed and said, "Let's stop a while, bro. I think we both got something to say to each other."

Antonio nodded. It was not natural to be acting as though nothing unusual was happening when two ace-boon[3] buddies were going to be blasting . . . each other within a few short days.

They rested their elbows on the railing separating them from the river. Antonio wiped his face with his short towel. The sunrise was now creating day.

Felix leaned heavily on the river's railing and stared across to the shores of Brooklyn. Finally, he broke the silence.

"Gee . . . man. I don't know how to come out with it."

Antonio helped. "It's about our fight, right?"

3. **ace-boon** [ās būn]: skilled, best (friends).

"Yeah, right." Felix's eyes squinted at the rising orange sun.

"I've been thinking about it too, *panin*.[4] In fact, since we found out it was going to be me and you, I've been awake at night, pulling punches on you, trying not to hurt you."

"Same here. It ain't natural not to think about the fight. I mean, we both are *cheverote*[5] fighters and we both want to win. But only one of us can win. There ain't no draws in the eliminations."

Felix tapped Antonio gently on the shoulder. "I don't mean to sound like I'm bragging, bro. But I wanna win, fair and square."

Antonio nodded quietly. "Yeah. We both know that in the ring the better man wins. Friend or no friend, brother or no . . ."

Felix finished it for him. "Brother. Tony, let's promise something right here. Okay?"

"If it's fair, *hermano*,[6] I'm for it." Antonio admired the courage of a tug boat pulling a barge five times its welterweight size.

"It's fair, Tony. When we get into the ring, it's gotta be like we never met. We gotta be like two heavy strangers that want the same thing and only one can have it. You understand, don'tcha?"

"*Sí*,[7] I know," Tony smiled. "No pulling punches. We go all the way."

"Yeah, that's right. Listen, Tony. Don't you think it's a good idea if we don't see each other until the day of the fight? I'm going to stay with my Aunt Lucy in the Bronx. I can use Gleason's Gym for working out. My manager says he got some sparring partners with more or less your style."

Tony scratched his nose pensively. "Yeah, it would be better for our heads." He held out his hand, palm upward. "Deal?"

"Deal." Felix lightly slapped open skin.

"Ready for some more running?" Tony asked lamely.

"Naw, bro. Let's cut it here. You go on. I kinda like to get things together in my head."

4. *panin* [pä′ nēn]: Spanish slang for "friend."
5. *cheverote* [chā vä rō′ tä]: Spanish slang for "cool dude."
6. *hermano* [ār mä′ nō]: Spanish for "brother."
7. *Sí* [sē]: Spanish for "Yes."

"You ain't worried, are you?" Tony asked.

"No way, man." Felix laughed out loud. "I got too much smarts for that. I just think it's cooler if we split right here. After the fight, we can get it together again like nothing ever happened."

The amigo brothers were not ashamed to hug each other tightly.

"Guess you're right. Watch yourself, Felix. I hear there's some pretty heavy dudes up in the Bronx. *Sauvecito*,[8] okay?"

"Okay. You watch yourself too, *sabe?*"[9]

Tony jogged away. Felix watched his friend disappear from view, throwing rights and lefts. Both fighters had a lot of psyching up to do before the big fight.

The days in training passed much too slowly. Although they kept out of each other's way, they were aware of each other's progress via the ghetto grapevine.

The evening before the big fight, Tony made his way to the roof of his tenement. In the quiet early dark, he peered over the ledge. Six stories below the lights of the city blinked and the sounds of cars mingled with the curses and the laughter of children in the street. He tried not to think of Felix, feeling he had succeeded in psyching his mind. But only in the ring would he really know. To spare Felix hurt, he would have to knock him out, early and quick.

Up in the South Bronx, Felix decided to take in a movie in an effort to keep Antonio's face away from his fists. The flick was *The Champion* with Kirk Douglas, the third time Felix was seeing it.

The champion was getting . . . beat, . . . his face being pounded into raw wet hamburger. His eyes were cut, jagged, bleeding, one eye swollen, the other almost shut. He was saved only by the sound of the bell.

Felix became the champ and Tony the challenger.

The movie audience was going out of its head, roaring in blood lust at the butchery going on. The champ hunched his shoulders grunting and sniffing red blood back into his broken nose. The challenger, confident that he had the championship in the bag,

---

8. *Sauvecito* [säü vā sē′ tō]: Spanish slang for "Take it easy."
9. *sabe* [sä′ bā]: Spanish slang for "You know?," or "Understand?"

threw a left. The champ countered with a dynamite right that exploded into the challenger's brains.

Felix's right arm felt the shock. Antonio's face, superimposed on the screen, was shattered and split apart by the awesome force of the killer blow. Felix saw himself in the ring, blasting Antonio against the ropes. The champ had to be forcibly restrained. The challenger was allowed to crumble slowly to the canvas, a broken bloody mess.

When Felix finally left the theater, he had figured out how to psyche himself for tomorrow's fight. It was Felix the Champion vs. Antonio the Challenger.

He walked up some dark streets, deserted except for small pockets of wary-looking kids wearing gang colors. Despite the fact that he was Puerto Rican like them, they eyed him as a stranger to their turf. Felix did a fast shuffle, bobbing and weaving, while letting loose a torrent of blows that would demolish whatever got in its way. It seemed to impress the brothers, who went about their own business.

Finding no takers, Felix decided to split to his aunt's. Walking the streets had not relaxed him, neither had the fight flick. All it had done was to stir him up. He let himself quietly into his Aunt Lucy's apartment and went straight to bed, falling into a fitful sleep with sounds of the gong for Round One.

Antonio was passing some heavy time on his rooftop. How would the fight tomorrow affect his relationship with Felix? After all, fighting was like any other profession. Friendship had nothing to do with it. A gnawing doubt crept in. He cut negative thinking real quick by doing some speedy fancy dance steps, bobbing and weaving like mercury. The night air was blurred with perpetual motions of left hooks and right crosses. Felix, his *amigo* brother, was not going to be Felix at all in the ring. Just an opponent with another face. Antonio went to sleep, hearing the opening bell for the first round. Like his friend in the South Bronx, he prayed for victory, via a quick clean knockout in the first round.

Large posters plastered all over the walls of local shops announced the fight between Antonio Cruz and Felix Vargas as the main bout.

The fight had created great interest in the neighborhood. Antonio and Felix were well liked and respected. Each had his own loyal following. Betting fever was high and ranged from a bottle of soda to cold hard cash on the line.

Antonio's fans bet with unbridled faith in his boxing skills. On the other side, Felix's admirers bet on his dynamite-packed fists.

Felix had returned to his apartment early in the morning of August 7th and stayed there, hoping to avoid seeing Antonio. He turned the radio on to *salsa* music[10] sounds and then tried to read while waiting for word from his manager.

The fight was scheduled to take place in Tompkins Square Park. It had been decided that the gymnasium of the Boys Club was not large enough to hold all the people who were sure to attend. In Tompkins Square Park, everyone who wanted could view the fight, whether from ringside or window fire escapes or tenement rooftops.

The morning of the fight Tompkins Square was a beehive of activity with numerous workers setting up the ring, the seats, and the guest speakers' stand. The scheduled bouts began shortly after noon and the park began filling up even earlier.

The local junior high school across from Tompkins Square Park served as the dressing room for all the fighters. Each was given a separate classroom with desk tops, covered with mats, serving as resting tables. Antonio thought he caught a glimpse of Felix waving to him from a room at the far end of the corridor. He waved back just in case it had been him.

The fighters changed from their street clothes into fighting gear. Antonio wore white trunks, black socks, and black shoes. Felix wore green trunks, white socks, and white boxing shoes. Each had dressing gowns to match their fighting trunks with their names neatly stitched on the back.

The loudspeakers blared into the open windows of the school. There were speeches by dignitaries, community leaders, and great boxers of yesteryear. Some were well prepared, some improvised on

10. *salsa* music [säl′ sä]: a popular kind of Hispanic music.

the spot. They all carried the same message of great pleasure and honor at being part of such a historic event. This great day was in the tradition of champions emerging from the streets of the lower east side.

Interwoven with the speeches were the sounds of the other boxing events. After the sixth bout, Felix was much relieved when his trainer Charlie said, "Time change. Quick knockout. This is it. We're on."

Waiting time was over. Felix was escorted from the classroom by a dozen fans in white T-shirts with the word FELIX across their fronts.

Antonio was escorted down a different stairwell and guided through a roped-off path.

As the two climbed into the ring, the crowd exploded with a roar. Antonio and Felix both bowed gracefully and then raised their arms in acknowledgment.

Antonio tried to be cool, but even as the roar was in its first birth, he turned slowly to meet Felix's eyes looking directly into his. Felix nodded his head and Antonio responded. And both as one, just as quickly, turned away to face his own corner.

Bong—bong—bong. The roar turned to stillness.

"Ladies and Gentlemen, *Señores y Señoras*."[11]

The announcer spoke slowly, pleased at his bilingual efforts.

"Now the moment we have all been waiting for—the main event between two fine young Puerto Rican fighters, products of our lower east side."

"*Loisaida*,"[12] called out a member of the audience.

"In this corner, weighing 134 pounds, Felix Vargas. And in this corner, weighing 133 pounds, Antonio Cruz. The winner will represent the Boys Club in the tournament of champions, the Golden Gloves. There will be no draw. May the best man win."

11. *Señores y Señoras* [sā nyō′ räs ē sā nyō′ räs]: Spanish for "Gentlemen and Ladies."
12. *Loisaida* [lō ē sī′ dä]: the way people in the neighborhood say "lower east sider."

The cheering of the crowd shook the window panes of the old buildings surrounding Tompkins Square Park. At the center of the ring, the referee was giving instructions to the youngsters.

"Keep your punches up. No low blows. No punching on the back of the head. Keep your heads up. Understand. Let's have a clean fight. Now shake hands and come out fighting."

Both youngsters touched gloves and nodded. They turned and danced quickly to their corners. Their head towels and dressing gowns were lifted neatly from their shoulders by the trainers' nimble fingers. Antonio crossed himself. Felix did the same.

BONG! BONG! ROUND ONE. Felix and Antonio turned and faced each other squarely in a fighting pose. Felix wasted no time. He came in fast, head low, half hunched toward his right shoulder, and lashed out with a straight left. He missed a right cross as Antonio slipped the punch and countered with one-two-three lefts that snapped Felix's head back, sending a mild shock coursing through him. If Felix had any small doubt about their friendship affecting their fight, it was being neatly dispelled.

Antonio danced, a joy to behold. His left hand was like a piston,[13] pumping jabs one right after another with seeming ease. Felix bobbed and weaved and never stopped boring in. He knew that at long range he was at a disadvantage. Antonio had too much reach on him. Only by coming in close could Felix hope to achieve the dreamed-of knockout.

Antonio knew the dynamite that was stored in his *amigo* brother's fist. He ducked a short right and missed a left hook. Felix trapped him against the ropes just long enough to pour some punishing rights and lefts to Antonio's hard midsection. Antonio slipped away from Felix, crashing two lefts to his head, which set Felix's right ear to ringing.

Bong! Both *amigos* froze a punch well on its way, sending up a roar of approval for good sportsmanship.

Felix walked briskly back to his corner. His right ear had not stopped ringing. Antonio gracefully danced his way toward his stool

---

13. **piston** [pis′ tən]: a cylinder that is quickly moved back and forth by the force of steam.

none the worse, except for glowing glove burns, showing angry red against the whiteness of his midribs.

"Watch that right, Tony." His trainer talked into his ear. "Remember Felix always goes to the body. He'll want you to drop your hands for his overhand left or right. Got it?"

Antonio nodded, sprayed water out between his teeth. He felt better as his sore midsection was being firmly rubbed.

Felix's corner was also busy.

"You gotta get in there, fella." Felix's trainer poured water over his curly Afro locks. "Get in there or he's gonna chop you up from way back."

Bong! Bong! Round two. Felix was off his stool and rushed Antonio like a bull, sending a hard right to his head. Beads of water exploded from Antonio's long hair.

Antonio, hurt, sent back a blurring barrage of lefts and rights that only meant pain to Felix, who returned with a short left to the head followed by a looping right to the body. Antonio countered with his own flurry, forcing Felix to give ground. But not for long.

Felix bobbed and weaved, bobbed and weaved, occasionally punching his two gloves together.

Antonio waited for the rush that was sure to come. Felix closed in and feinted with his left shoulder and threw his right instead. Lights suddenly exploded inside Felix's head as Antonio slipped the blow and hit him with a pistonlike left, catching him flush on the point of his chin.

Bedlam broke loose as Felix's legs momentarily buckled. He fought off a series of rights and lefts and came back with a strong right that taught Antonio respect.

Antonio danced in carefully. He knew Felix had the habit of playing possum when hurt, to sucker an opponent within reach of the powerful bombs he carried in each fist.

A right to the head slowed Antonio's pretty dancing. He answered with his own left at Felix's right eye that began puffing up within three seconds.

Antonio, a bit too eager, moved in too close and Felix had him entangled into a rip-roaring, punching toe-to-toe slugfest that brought the whole Tompkins Square Park screaming to its feet.

Rights to the body. Lefts to the head. Neither fighter was giving an inch. Suddenly a short right caught Antonio squarely on the chin. His long legs turned to jelly and his arms flailed out desperately. Felix, grunting like a bull, threw wild punches from every direction. Antonio, groggy, bobbed and weaved, evading most of the blows. Suddenly his head cleared. His left flashed out hard and straight catching Felix on the bridge of his nose.

Felix lashed back with a haymaker, right off the ghetto streets. At the same instant, his eye caught another left hook from Antonio. Felix swung out trying to clear the pain. Only the frenzied screaming of those along ringside let him know that he had dropped Antonio. Fighting off the growing haze, Antonio struggled to his feet, got up, ducked, and threw a smashing right that dropped Felix flat on his back.

Felix got up as fast as he could in his own corner, groggy but still game. He didn't even hear the count. In a fog, he heard the roaring of the crowd, who seemed to have gone insane. His head cleared to hear the bell sound at the end of the round. He was . . . glad. His trainer sat him down on the stool.

In his corner, Antonio was doing what all fighters do when they are hurt. They sit and smile at everyone.

The referee signaled the ring doctor to check the fighters out. He did so and then gave his okay. The cold water sponges brought clarity to both *amigo* brothers. They were rubbed until their circulation ran free.

Bong! Round three—the final round. Up to now it had been tic-tac-toe, pretty much even. But everyone knew there could be no draw and that this round would decide the winner.

This time, to Felix's surprise, it was Antonio who came out fast, charging across the ring. Felix braced himself but couldn't ward off the barrage of punches. Antonio drove Felix hard against the ropes.

The crowd ate it up. Thus far the two had fought with *mucho corazón*.[14] Felix tapped his gloves and commenced his attack anew. Antonio, throwing boxer's caution to the winds, jumped in to meet him.

14. **mucho corazón** [mü′ chō kō rä sōn′]: Spanish for courage; literally, "a lot of heart."

Both pounded away. Neither gave an inch and neither fell to the canvas. Felix's left eye was tightly closed. Claret red blood poured from Antonio's nose. They fought toe-to-toe.

The sounds of their blows were loud in contrast to the silence of a crowd gone completely mute. The referee was stunned by their savagery.

Bong! Bong! Bong! The bell sounded over and over again. Felix and Antonio were past hearing. Their blows continued to pound on each other like hailstones.

Finally the referee and the two trainers pried Felix and Antonio apart. Cold water was poured over them to bring them back to their senses.

They looked around and then rushed toward each other. A cry of alarm surged through Tompkins Square Park. Was this a fight to the death instead of a boxing match?

The fear soon gave way to wave upon wave of cheering as the two *amigos* embraced.

No matter what the decision, they knew they would always be champions to each other.

BONG! BONG! BONG! "Ladies and Gentlemen. *Señores* and *Señoras*. The winner and representative to the Golden Gloves Tournament of Champions is . . ."

The announcer turned to point to the winner and found himself alone. Arm in arm the champions had already left the ring.

PIRI THOMAS

Piri Thomas was born in 1928 and grew up in New York City. Thomas's adult life did not begin well. At twenty-two, he was sent to prison for attempted armed robbery. In prison, he began to write. Four years later, after he was released, all his written work was accidentally destroyed. Back in the community, Thomas became involved in drug rehabilitation programs—and began writing again.

Much of Thomas's writing is autobiographical and makes use of the dialect of Spanish Harlem in New York. "Amigo Brothers" is from his book, *Stories from the Barrio*.

Hannah Armstrong

EDGAR LEE MASTERS

I wrote him a letter asking him for old times' sake
To discharge[1] my sick boy from the army;
But maybe he couldn't read it.
Then I went to town and had James Garber,
Who wrote beautifully, write him a letter;   5
But maybe that was lost in the mails.
So I traveled all the way to Washington.
I was more than an hour finding the White House.
And when I found it they turned me away,
Hiding their smiles. Then I thought: 10
"Oh, well, he ain't the same as when I boarded him
And he and my husband worked together
And all of us called him Abe, there in Menard."
As a last attempt I turned to a guard and said:
"Please say it's old Aunt Hannah Armstrong   15
From Illinois, come to see him about her sick boy
In the army."
Well, just in a moment they let me in!
And when he saw me he broke in a laugh,
And dropped his business as president,   20
And wrote in his own hand Doug's discharge,
Talking the while of the early days,
And telling stories.

1. **discharge:** [dis chärj´]: release, let go.

The Great Good Man Marsden Hartley, 1942, oil on masonite, 40" x 30", Museum of Fine Arts, Boston

E D G A R   L E E   M A S T E R S

Edgar Lee Masters [1868-1950] was born in Garnett, Kansas, but grew up in the small Illinois towns of Petersburg and Lewistown. First he became a lawyer. Later, when he became a poet, he used a variety of pseudonyms to keep his literary life separate from his law practice.

Masters is best known for his *Spoon River Anthology*, which began as a novel about the kinds of people he knew in small-town Illinois. Following the example of the *Greek Anthology*, a collection of ancient Greek poems in which the dead comment on their own lives, Masters's characters in *Spoon River Anthology* are dead and each narrates his or her life story.

Hannah Armstrong **67**

Graduates hear some Clinton advice

ASSOCIATED PRESS

WASHINGTON—President Clinton told new college graduates yesterday to "assume more personal responsibility" in the nation's future without losing sight of their personal priorities. "Always save time for your friends," he advised.

Speaking by telephone to a commencement audience at William Jewell College in Liberty, Mo., Clinton accepted an honorary doctorate.[1] His goddaughter, Sarah Staley of Little Rock, Ark., was among the graduates.

"I want to urge all who are here listening to me today to look out at the great adventures of your life and to seize them, but also to always save time for your friends," he said.

Clinton said one of the first things he did as president-elect was visit the home of Sarah's mother, Carolyn Staley, one of Clinton's oldest friends, who played host to a gathering of his pals.

"Amid life's challenges and disappointments, your friends are an anchor in a storm, and I urge you to keep them," the president said in the brief remarks.

1. **honorary doctorate** [on′ ə rer′ ē dok′ tər it]: a university doctor's degree given as an honor rather than earned through regular studies.

LOB'S GIRL

JOAN AIKEN

Some people choose their dogs, and some dogs choose their people. The Pengelly family had no say in the choosing of Lob; he came to them in the second way, and very decisively.

It began on the beach, the summer when Sandy was five, Don, her older brother, twelve, and the twins were three. Sandy was really Alexandra, because her grandmother had a beautiful picture of a queen in a diamond tiara[1] and high collar of pearls. It hung by Granny Pearce's kitchen sink and was as familiar as the doormat. When Sandy was born everyone agreed that she was the living spit of the picture, and so she was called Alexandra and Sandy for short.

On this summer day she was lying peacefully reading a comic and not keeping an eye on the twins, who didn't need it because they were occupied in seeing which of them could wrap the most seaweed around the other one's legs. Father—Bert Pengelly—and Don were up

1. **tiara** [tē er′ ə]: a band of gold, jewels, or flowers worn around the head as an ornament.

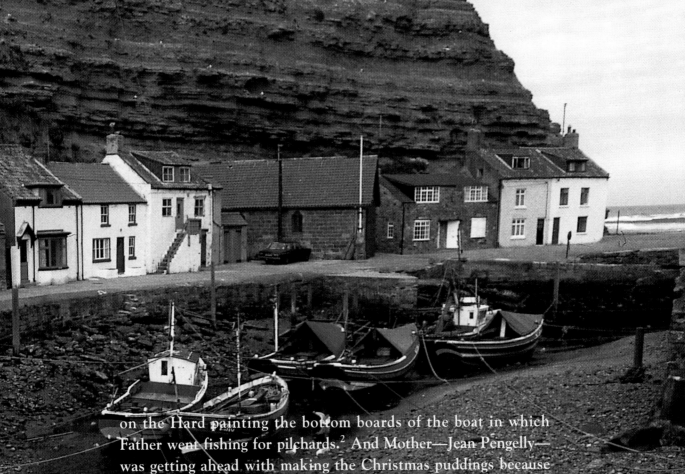

on the Hard painting the bottom boards of the boat in which
Father went fishing for pilchards.[2] And Mother—Jean Pengelly—
was getting ahead with making the Christmas puddings because
she never felt easy in her mind if they weren't made and safely put
away by the end of August. As usual, each member of the family
was happily getting on with his or her own affairs. Little did they
guess how soon this state of things would be changed by the large
new member who was going to erupt into their midst.

Sandy rolled onto her back to make sure that the twins were
not climbing on slippery rocks or getting cut off by the tide. At the
same moment a large body struck her forcibly in the midriff and
she was covered by flying sand. Instinctively she shut her eyes and
felt the sand being wiped off her face by something that seemed
like a warm, rough, damp flannel. She opened her eyes and looked.
It was a tongue. Its owner was a large and bouncy young Alsatian,

2. **pilchards** [pil' chərdz]: small fish related to herrings.

or German shepherd, with topaz[3] eyes, black-tipped prick ears, a thick, soft coat, and a bushy black-tipped tail.

"*Lob!*" shouted a man farther up the beach. "Lob, come here!"

But Lob, as if trying to atone[4] for the surprise he had given her, went on licking the sand off Sandy's face, wagging his tail so hard while he kept on knocking up more clouds of sand. His owner, a gray-haired man with a limp, walked over as quickly as he could and seized him by the collar.

"I hope he didn't give you a fright?" the man said to Sandy. "He meant it in play—he's only young."

"Oh, no, I think he's *beautiful,*" said Sandy truly. She picked up a bit of driftwood and threw it. Lob, whisking easily out of his master's grip, was after it like a sand-colored bullet. He came back with the stick, beaming, and gave it to Sandy. At the same time he gave himself, though no one else was aware of this at the time. But with Sandy, too, it was love at first sight, and when, after a lot more stick-throwing, she and the twins joined Father and Don to go home for tea, they cast many a backward glance at Lob being led firmly away by his master.

"I wish we could play with him every day." Tess sighed.

"Why can't we?" said Tim.

Sandy explained. "Because Mr. Dodsworth, who owns him, is from Liverpool, and he is only staying at the Fisherman's Arms till Saturday."

"Is Liverpool a long way off?"

"Right at the other end of England from Cornwall, I'm afraid."

It was a Cornish fishing village where the Pengelly family lived, with rocks and cliffs and a strip of beach and a little round harbor, and palm trees growing in the gardens of the little whitewashed stone houses. The village was approached by a narrow, steep, twisting hill-road, and guarded by a notice that said LOW GEAR FOR 1 1/2 MILES, DANGEROUS TO CYCLISTS.

3. **topaz** [tō′ paz]: golden brown.
4. **atone** [ə tōn′]: make up for.

The Pengelly children went home to scones[5] with Cornish cream and jam, thinking they had seen the last of Lob. But they were much mistaken. The whole family was playing cards by the fire in the front room after supper when there was a loud thump and a crash of china in the kitchen.

"My Christmas puddings!" exclaimed Jean, and ran out.

"Did you put TNT[6] in them, then?" her husband said.

But it was Lob, who, finding the front door shut, had gone around to the back and bounced in through the open kitchen window, where the puddings were cooling on the sill. Luckily only the smallest was knocked down and broken.

Lob stood on his hind legs and plastered Sandy's face with licks. Then he did the same for the twins, who shrieked with joy.

"Where does this friend of yours come from?" inquired Mr. Pengelly.

"He's staying at the Fisherman's Arms—I mean his owner is."

"Then he must go back there. Find a bit of string, Sandy, to tie to his collar."

"I wonder how he found his way here," Mrs. Pengelly said, when the reluctant Lob had been led whining away and Sandy had explained about their afternoon's game on the beach. "Fisherman's Arms is right round the other side of the harbor."

Lob's owner scolded him and thanked Mr. Pengelly for bringing him back. Jean Pengelly warned the children that they had better not encourage Lob any more if they met him on the beach, or it would only lead to more trouble. So they dutifully took no notice of him the next day until he spoiled their good resolutions[7] by dashing up to them with joyful barks, wagging his tail so hard that he winded Tess and knocked Tim's legs from under him.

They had a happy day, playing on the sand.

The next day was Saturday. Sandy had found out that Mr. Dodsworth was to catch the half-past-nine train. She went out

5. **scones** [skōnz]: thick, round biscuits.
6. **TNT:** a yellow-colored solid used as an explosive.
7. **resolutions** [rez′ ə lü′ shənz]: decisions or intentions.

secretly, down to the station, nodded to Mr. Hoskins, the station-master, who wouldn't dream of charging any local[8] for a platform ticket, and climbed up on the footbridge that led over the tracks. She didn't want to be seen, but she did want to see. She saw Mr. Dodsworth get on the train, accompanied by an unhappy-looking Lob with drooping ears and tail. Then she saw the train slide away out sight around the next headland,[9] with a melancholy wail that sounded like Lob's last good-bye.

Sandy wished she hadn't had the idea of coming to the station. She walked home miserably, with her shoulders hunched and her hands in her pockets. For the rest of the day she was so cross and un-like herself that Tess and Tim were quite surprised, and her mother gave her a dose of senna.[10]

A week passed. Then, one evening, Mrs. Pengelly and the younger children were in the front room playing snakes and tadders. Mr. Pengelly and Don had gone fishing on the evening tide. If your father is a fisherman, he will never be home at the same time from one week to the next.

Suddenly, history repeating itself, there was a crash from the kitchen. Jean Pengelly leaped up, crying, "My blackberry jelly!" She and the children had spent the morning picking and the afternoon boiling fruit.

But Sandy was ahead of her mother. With flushed cheeks and eyes like stars she had darted into the kitchen, where she and Lob were hugging one another in a frenzy of joy. About a yard of his tongue was out, and he was licking every part of her that he could reach.

"Good heavens!" exclaimed Jean. "How in the world did *he* get here?"

"He must have walked," said Sandy. "Look at his feet."

They were worn, dusty, and tarry.[11] One had a cut on the pad.

---

8. **local** [lō′ kəl]: local resident or person native to the area.
9. **headland:** a point of high land jutting into a body of water.
10. **senna** [sen′ ə]: dried leaves used as an herbal medicine.
11. **tarry** [tär′ ē]: covered with tar.

"They ought to be bathed," said Jean Pengelly. "Sandy, run a bowl of warm water while I get the disinfectant."[12]

"What'll we do about him, Mother?" said Sandy anxiously.

Mrs. Pengelly looked at her daughter's pleading eyes and sighed.

"He must go back to his owner, of course," she said, making her voice firm. "Your dad can get the address from the Fisherman's tomorrow, and phone him or send a telegram. In the meantime he'd better have a long drink and a good meal."

Lob was very grateful for the drink and the meal, and made no objection to having his feet washed. Then he flopped down on the hearthrug and slept in front of the fire they had lit because it was a cold, wet evening, with his head on Sandy's feet. He was a very tired dog. He had walked all the way from Liverpool to Cornwall, which is more than four hundred miles.

The next day Mr. Pengelly phoned Lob's owner, and the following morning Mr. Dodsworth arrived off the night train, decidedly put out, to take his pet home. That parting was worse than the first. Lob whined, Don walked out of the house, the twins burst out crying, and Sandy crept up to her bedroom afterward and lay with her face pressed into the quilt, feeling as if she were bruised all over.

Jean Pengelly took them all into Plymouth to see the circus on the next day and the twins cheered up a little, but even the hour's ride in the train each way and the Liberty horses and performing seals could not cure Sandy's sore heart.

She need not have bothered, though. In ten days' time Lob was back—limping this time, with a torn ear and a patch missing out of his furry coat, as if he had met and tangled with an enemy or two in the course of his four-hundred-mile walk.

Bert Pengelly rang up Liverpool again. Mr. Dodsworth, when he answered, sounded weary. He said, "That dog has already cost me two days that I can't spare away from my work—plus endless time in police stations and drafting newspaper advertisements. I'm too old

12. **disinfectant** [dis′ in fek′ tənt]: a substance that destroys germs and may prevent infection.

for these ups and downs. I think we'd better face the fact, Mr. Pengelly, that it's your family he wants to stay with—that is, if you want to have him."

Bert Pengelly gulped. He was not a rich man; and Lob was a pedigreed[13] dog. He said cautiously, "How much would you be asking for him?"

"Good heavens, man, I'm not suggesting I'd *sell* him to you. You must have him as a gift. Think of the train fares I'll be saving. You'll be doing me a good turn."

"Is he a big eater?" Bert asked doubtfully.

By this time the children, breathless in the background listening to one side of this conversation, had realized what was in the wind and were dancing up and down with their hands clasped beseechingly.[14]

"Oh, not for his size," Lob's owner assured Bert. "Two or three pounds of meat a day and some vegetables and gravy and biscuits—he does very well on that."

Alexandra's father looked over the telephone at his daughter's swimming eyes and trembling lips. He reached a decision. "Well, then, Mr. Dodsworth," he said briskly, "we'll accept your offer and thank you very much. The children will be overjoyed and you can be sure Lob has come to a good home. They'll look after him and see he gets enough exercise. But I can tell you," he ended firmly, "if he wants to settle in with us he'll have to learn to eat a lot of fish."

So that was how Lob came to live with the Pengelly family. Everybody loved him and he loved them all. But there was never any question who came first with him. He was Sandy's dog. He slept by her bed and followed her everywhere he was allowed.

Nine years went by, and each summer Mr. Dodsworth came back to stay at the Fisherman's Arms and call on his erstwhile[15] dog. Lob always met him with recognition and dignified pleasure, accompanied

13. **pedigreed** [ped′ ə grēd]: having record of breeding or ancestry.
14. **beseechingly** [bi sēch′ ing lē]: as though asking or begging.
15. **erstwhile** [ėrst′ hwīl]: former, past.

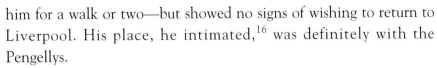

him for a walk or two—but showed no signs of wishing to return to Liverpool. His place, he intimated,[16] was definitely with the Pengellys.

In the course of nine years Lob changed less than Sandy. As she went into her teens he became a little slower, a little stiffer, there was a touch of gray on his nose, but he was still a handsome dog. He and Sandy still loved one another devotedly.

One evening in October all the summer visitors had left, and the little fishing town looked empty and secretive. It was a wet, windy dusk. When the children came home from school—even the twins were at high school now, and Don was a full-fledged fisherman—Jean Pengelly said, "Sandy, your Aunt Rebecca says she's lonesome because Uncle Will Hoskins has gone out trawling,[17] and she wants one of you to go and spend the evening with her. You go, dear; you can take your homework with you."

Sandy looked far from enthusiastic.

"Can I take Lob with me?"

"You know Aunt Becky doesn't really like dogs—Oh, very well." Mrs. Pengelly sighed. "I suppose she'll have to put up with him as well as you."

Reluctantly Sandy tidied herself, took her schoolbag, put on the damp raincoat she had just taken off, fastened Lob's lead to his collar, and set off to walk through the dusk to Aunt Becky's cottage, which was five minutes' climb up the steep hill.

The wind was howling through the shrouds[18] of boats drawn up on the Hard.

"Put some cheerful music on, do," said Jean Pengelly to the nearest twin. "Anything to drown that wretched sound while I make your dad's supper." So Don, who had just come in, put on some rock music, loud. Which was why the Pengellys did not hear the truck hurtle down the hill and crash against the post office wall a few minutes later.

16. **intimated** [in′ tə māt əd]: hinted.
17. **trawling** [trôl′ ing]: fishing with a net.
18. **shrouds** [shrouds]: coverings made of cloth or some protective material.

Dr. Travers was driving through Cornwall with his wife, taking a late holiday before patients began coming down with winter colds and flu. He saw the sign that said STEEP HILL. LOW GEAR FOR 1 1/2 MILES. Dutifully he changed into second gear.

"We must be nearly there," said his wife, looking out of her window. "I noticed a sign on the coast road that said the Fisherman's Arms was two miles. What a narrow, dangerous hill! But the cottages are very pretty—Oh, Frank, stop, *stop!* There's a child, I'm sure it's a child—by the wall over there!"

Dr. Travers jammed on his brakes and brought the car to a stop. A little stream ran down by the road in a shallow stone culvert,[19] and half in the water lay something that looked, in the dusk, like a pile of clothes—or was it the body of a child? Mrs. Travers was out of the car in a flash, but her husband was quicker.

"Don't touch her, Emily!" he said sharply. "She's been hit. Can't be more than a few minutes. Remember that truck that overtook us half a mile back, speeding like the devil? Here, quick, go into that cottage and phone for an ambulance. The girl's in a bad way. I'll stay here and do what I can to stop the bleeding. Don't waste a minute."

Doctors are expert at stopping dangerous bleeding, for they know the right places to press. This Dr. Travers was able to do, but he didn't dare do more; the girl was lying in a queerly crumpled heap, and he guessed she had a number of bones broken and that it would be highly dangerous to move her. He watched her with great concentration, wondering where the truck had got to and what other damage it had done.

Mrs. Travers was very quick. She had seen plenty of accident cases and knew the importance of speed. The first cottage she tried had a phone; in four minutes she was back, and in six an ambulance was wailing down the hill.

Its attendants lifted the child onto a stretcher as carefully as if she were made of fine thistledown.[20] The ambulance sped off to

---

19. **culvert** [kul′ vərt]: a small channel or drain.
20. **thistledown** [this′ əl doun′]: soft, feathery fluff from thistle seeds.

Plymouth—for the local cottage hospital did not take serious accident cases—and Dr. Travers went down to the police station to report what he had done.

He found that the police already knew about the speeding truck—which had suffered from loss of brakes and ended up with its radiator halfway through the post-office wall. The driver was concussed[21] and shocked, but the police thought he was the only person injured—until Dr. Travers told his tale.

At half-past nine that night Aunt Rebecca Hoskins was sitting by her fire thinking aggrieved thoughts about the inconsiderateness of nieces who were asked to supper and never turned up, when she was startled by a neighbor, who burst in, exclaiming, "Have you heard about Sandy Pengelly, then, Mrs. Hoskins? Terrible thing, poor little soul, and they don't know if she's likely to live. Police have got the truck driver that hit her—ah, it didn't ought to be allowed, speeding through the place like that at umpty miles an hour, they ought to jail him for life—not that that'd be any comfort to poor Bert and Jean."

Horrified, Aunt Rebecca put on a coat and went down to her brother's house. She found the family with white shocked faces; Bert and Jean were about to drive off to the hospital where Sandy had been taken, and the twins were crying bitterly. Lob was nowhere to be seen. But Aunt Rebecca was not interested in dogs; she did not inquire about him.

"Thank the lord you've come, Beck," said her brother. "Will you stay the night with Don and the twins? Don's out looking for Lob and heaven knows when we'll be back; we may get a bed with Jean's mother in Plymouth."

"Oh, if only I'd never invited the poor child," wailed Mrs. Hoskins. But Bert and Jean hardly heard her.

That night seemed to last forever. The twins cried themselves to sleep. Don came home very late and grim-faced. Bert and Jean sat in a waiting room of the Western Counties Hospital, but Sandy was

21. **concussed** [kən kusd′]: injured in the head by a blow.

unconscious, they were told, and she remained so. All that could be done for her was done. She was given transfusions to replace all the blood she had lost. The broken bones were set and put in slings and cradles.

"Is she a healthy girl? Has she a good constitution?"[22] the emergency doctor asked.

"Aye, doctor, she is that," Bert said hoarsely. The lump in Jean's throat prevented her from answering; she merely nodded.

"Then she ought to have a chance. But I won't conceal from you that her condition is very serious, unless she shows signs of coming out from this coma."

But as hour succeeded hour, Sandy showed no signs of recovering consciousness. Her parents sat in the waiting room with haggard faces; sometimes one of them would go to telephone the family at home, or to try to get a little sleep at the home of Granny Pearce, not far away.

At noon next day Dr. and Mrs. Travers went to the Pengelly cottage to inquire how Sandy was doing, but the report was gloomy: "Still in a very serious condition." The twins were miserably unhappy. They forgot that they had sometimes called their elder sister bossy and only remembered how often she had shared her pocket money with them, how she read to them and took them for picnics and helped with their homework. Now there was no Sandy, no Mother and Dad, Don went around with a gray, shuttered face, and worse still, there was no Lob.

The Western Counties Hospital is a large one, with dozens of different departments and five or six connected buildings, each with three or four entrances. By that afternoon it became noticeable that a dog seemed to have taken up position outside the hospital, with the fixed intention of getting in. Patiently he would try first one entrance and then another, all the way around, and then begin again. Sometimes he would get a little way inside, following a visitor, but animals were, of course, forbidden, and he was always kindly but

22. **constitution**: [kon′ stə tü′ shən]: nature or makeup.

firmly turned out again. Sometimes the guard at the main entrance gave him a pat or offered him a bit of sandwich—he looked so wet and beseeching and desperate. But he never ate the sandwich. No one seemed to own him or to know where he came from; Plymouth is a large city and he might have belonged to anybody.

At tea time Granny Pearce came through the pouring rain to bring a flask of hot tea with brandy in it to her daughter and son-in-law. Just as she reached the main entrance the guard was gently but forcibly shoving out a large, agitated, soaking-wet Alsatian dog.

"No, old fellow, you can *not* come in. Hospitals are for people, not for dogs."

"Why, bless me," exclaimed old Mrs. Pearce. "That's Lob! Here, Lob, Lobby boy!"

Lob ran to her, whining. Mrs. Pearce walked up to the desk.

"I'm sorry, madam, you can't bring that dog in here," the guard said.

Mrs. Pearce was a very determined old lady. She looked the porter in the eye.

"Now, see here, young man. That dog has walked twenty miles from St. Killan to get to my granddaughter. Heaven knows how he knew she was here, but it's plain he knows. And he ought to have his rights! He ought to get to see her! Do you know," she went on, bristling, "that dog has walked the length of England—*twice*—to be with that girl? And you think you can keep him out with your fiddling rules and regulations?"

"I'll have to ask the medical officer," the guard said weakly.

"You do that, young man." Granny Pearce sat down in a determined manner, shutting her umbrella, and Lob sat patiently dripping at her feet. Every now and then he shook his head, as if to dislodge something heavy that was tied around his neck.

Presently a tired, thin, intelligent-looking man in a white coat came downstairs, with an impressive, silver-haired man in a dark suit, and there was a low-voiced discussion. Granny Pearce eyed them, biding her time.

"Frankly . . . not much to lose," said the older man. The man in the white coat approached Granny Pearce.

"It's strictly against every rule, but as it's such a serious case we are making an exception," he said to her quietly. "But only *outside* her bedroom door—and only for a moment or two."

Without a word, Granny Pearce rose and stumped upstairs. Lob followed close to her skirts, as if he knew his hope lay with her.

They waited in the green-floored corridor outside Sandy's room. The door was half shut. Bert and Jean were inside. Everything was terribly quiet. A nurse came out. The white-coated man asked her something and she shook her head. She had left the door ajar and through it could now be seen a high, narrow bed with a lot of gadgets around it. Sandy lay there, very flat under the covers, very still. Her head was turned away. All Lob's attention was riveted[23] on the bed. He strained toward it, but Granny Pearce clasped his collar firmly.

"I've done a lot for you, my boy, now you behave yourself," she whispered grimly. Lob let out a faint whine, anxious and pleading.

At the sound of that whine Sandy stirred just a little. She sighed and moved her head the least fraction. Lob whined again. And then Sandy turned her head right over. Her eyes opened, looking at the door.

"Lob?" she murmured—no more than a breath of sound. "Lobby, boy?"

The doctor by Granny Pearce drew a quick, sharp breath. Sandy moved her left arm—the one that was not broken—from below the covers and let her hand dangle down feeling as she always did in the mornings, for Lob's furry head. The doctor nodded slowly.

"All right," he whispered. "Let him go to the bedside. But keep a hold of him."

Granny Pearce and Lob moved to the bedside. Now she could see Bert and Jean, white-faced and shocked, on the far side of the bed. But she didn't look at them. She looked at the smile on her granddaughter's face as the groping fingers found Lob's wet ears and gently pulled them. "Good boy," whispered Sandy, and fell asleep again.

Granny Pearce led Lob out into the passage again. There she let go of him and he ran off swiftly down the stairs. She would have

23. **riveted** [riv′ it əd]: fixed firmly.

followed him, but Bert and Jean had come out into the passage, and she spoke to Bert fiercely.

"*I* don't know why you were so foolish as not to bring the dog before! Leaving him to find the way here himself—"

"But, Mother!" said Jean Pengelly. "That can't have been Lob. What a chance to take! Suppose Sandy hadn't—" She stopped, with her handkerchief pressed to her mouth.

"Not Lob? I've known that dog nine years! I suppose I ought to know my own granddaughter's dog?"

"Listen, Mother," said Bert. "Lob was killed by the same truck that hit Sandy. Don found him—when he went to look for Sandy's schoolbag. He was—he was dead. Ribs all smashed. No question of that. Don told me on the phone—he and Will Hoskins rowed a half mile out to sea and sank the dog with a lump of concrete tied to his collar. Poor old boy. Still—he was getting on. Couldn't have lasted forever."

"*Sank him at sea?* Then what—?"

Slowly old Mrs. Pearce, and then the other two, turned to look at the trail of dripping-wet footprints that led down the hospital stairs.

In the Pengellys' garden they have a stone, under the palm tree. It says: "Lob. Sandy's dog. Buried at sea."

JOAN AIKEN

Joan Aiken was born in England in 1924. She started writing stories and poems on "huge two-shilling writing blocks" when she was only five. When Aiken was seventeen, the British Broadcasting Corporation chose one of her stories to broadcast on their children's hour.

At different times, Aiken worked for the BBC, the United Nations Information Service, and *Argosy* magazine. At the age of thirty, when she was a widow with two small children, Aiken began writing steadily to support her family. She has written a dozen thrillers for adults and more than twenty books for young people, including *The Wolves of Willoughby Close* and *The Whispering Mountain*.

The CHINESE CHECKER PLAYERS

Richard Brautigan

When I was six years old
I played Chinese checkers[1]
   with a woman
who was ninety-three years old.
She lived by herself   5
in an apartment down the hall
   from ours.
We played Chinese checkers
every Monday and Thursday nights.
While we played she usually talked   10
about her husband
who had been dead for seventy years,
and we drank tea and ate cookies
   and cheated.

Marbles V Charles Bell, 1982, oil on canvas, 48″ x 84 ¹/₂″

1. **Chinese checkers:** a game similar to checkers in which marbles are used on a board with holes.

RICHARD BRAUTIGAN

Richard Brautigan [1935-1984] was born in Spokane, Washington. For many years he made a living solely from writing poetry and novels, until he became an instructor at Montana State University. His first book of poems was published when he was twenty-two.

In all his work, Brautigan wrote about life and nature and poked fun at both. One interesting collection is made up of eight poems, each printed on a separate seed packet envelope, and is called *Please Plant This Book*.

MR.MISENHEIMER'S GARDEN

CHARLES KURALT

We've been wandering the back roads since 1967, and we've been to a few places we'll never forget. One of them was on Route 10, Surry County, Virginia. We rolled in here on a day in the spring of 1972 thinking this was another of those little roadside rest stops. But there were flowers on the picnic tables. That was the first surprise.

And beyond the tables, we found a paradise, a beautiful garden of thirteen acres, bright with azaleas, thousands of them, and bordered by dogwoods in bloom, and laced by a mile of paths in the shade of tall pines. In all our travels, it was the loveliest garden I'd ever seen. It made me wonder how large a battalion[1] of state-employed gardeners it took to keep the place up. The answer was it took one old man, and he was nobody's employee. Walter Misenheimer, a retired nurseryman,[2] created all this in the woods next to his house, created it alone after he retired at the age of seventy. He was eighty-three when I met him and was spending every day tending his garden for the pleasure of strangers who happened to stop.

Walter Misenheimer: I like people, and this is my way of following out some of the teachings of my parents. When I was a youngster, one of the things they said was, "If you don't try to make the world just a little bit nicer when you leave here, what is the reason for man's existence in the first place?" I have tried to give it to the state. The Parks Department says it is too small for them. The Highway Department says it is too big for them.

1. **battalion** [bə talʼ yən]: a large group of people with a common purpose.
2. **nurseryman** [nėrʼ sər ē mən]: person who grows or sells young trees and plants.

Kuralt: What's going to happen to this place after you're gone?

Misenheimer: Well, I imagine that within a very few years, this will be undergrowth, or nature will take it over again.

Kuralt: You mean, it's not going to survive?

Misenheimer: I doubt it.

Kuralt: That's a terribly discouraging thing, isn't it?

Misenheimer: Well, that's the way I see it now.

We watched for a while as people enjoyed the beauty of Walter Misenheimer's garden. And we left, and a few years later somebody sent me a clipping from the Surry County paper. It said Walter Misenheimer had died. I wondered what would happen to his garden. I wondered whether the Virginia sun still lights the branches of the dogwood, which he planted there.

Well, it does. Some stories have happy endings. Walter Misenheimer's garden does survive, and so does his spirit, in Haeja Namkoong. It seems that she stopped by the garden just a few months after we did, eleven years ago.

Haeja Namkoong: We slowed down and saw a sign and picnic tables and a lot of flowers blooming. We came to the picnic table, found a water spigot, helped ourselves, and we were sort of curious as to what this place was all about. Finally, we saw the old man sort of wobbling around and coming 'cross the lawn, saying "Hello," and just waving to us to stop. I guess he was afraid we were going to leave.

To please the old man, and herself, Haeja Namkoong stayed the afternoon with him, walking in his garden. It made her remember, she says, something she wanted once.

Haeja: I grew up in a large city in Korea, and I have never really seen rice grow. I always dreamed about living in the country, about a small, little cabin in the wilderness, with lots of flowers. That's what I dreamed about, but I guess that was just childhood dreams.

When the sun went down that day, the young woman said good-bye to the old man and headed home to Boston, but the roadside Eden called her back. That is, Walter Misenheimer did. He phoned her, long distance, and asked her to come for a little while and help in the garden.

Haeja: He was sort of pleading with me, "Please come down. Just help me for a couple of weeks."

A couple of weeks only, and then a few more, and then it was Christmas. Haeja Namkoong was twenty-six. She had no family. Neither did Walter Misenheimer and his wife.

Haeja: From wildflowers to man-grown shrubberies, he taught me. I was interested in learning the whole thing. I was out here almost every day with him.

They became as father and daughter working in the garden, and in time Haeja Namkoong was married in the garden.

Haeja: He was very proud to give me away. I guess he never thought, since he didn't have any children of his own, he would give someone away.

Brown earth was coaxed by the gentle old man into green growth and flowering red and pink and white. The earth rewards every loving attention it is paid. People repay such love, too, in memory.

Haeja: I was very, very close to my mother. But other than my mother, I can't remember anyone that loved me so much and cared for me so much as Mr. Misenheimer.

The garden is still here. Walter Misenheimer died in 1979 and left it to Haeja Namkoong. She pays a caretaker, Ed Trible, to help keep it beautiful for anybody who passes by. Haeja and her husband and their children live in Richmond now, but they return on weekends to work in the garden.

Haeja: So, knowing how much the garden meant to him, I want to keep it up and carry on.

Walter Misenheimer told me that he expected when he was gone the garden would soon be overgrown. He might have known better. His garden shows that something grows from seeds and cultivation. And if what you plant is love and kindness, something grows from that, too.

Haeja: Look at this purple one.
Child: I like the red.
Haeja: Aren't they pretty?

CHARLES KURALT

Charles Kuralt was born in 1934 in Wilmington, North Carolina. After attending college there, he became a reporter for the *Charlotte News* in Charlotte, North Carolina. When he moved to New York City to work as a writer and correspondent for CBS News, he began to travel.

For the television feature "On the Road," Kuralt began a long career of traveling America's back roads in search of off-beat stories. With a camera and sound crew, Kuralt has averaged 50,000 miles a year, looking for—and finding—interesting, ordinary people. These stories of people who have quiet, productive lives in a noisy, troubled world help prove, Kuralt says, that "people go on living their lives in spite of big black headlines."

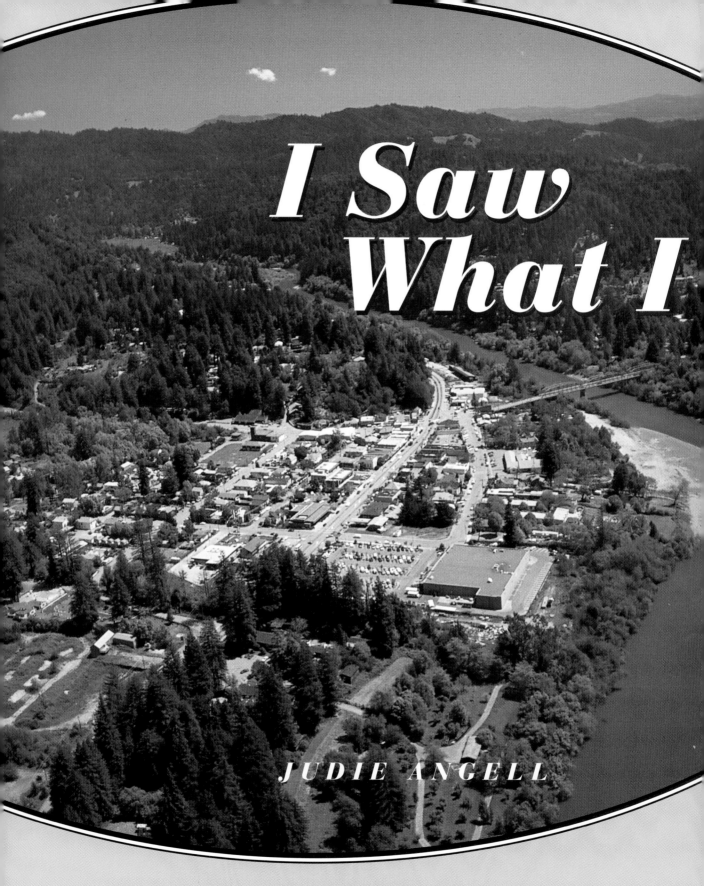

I Saw What I

JUDIE ANGELL

Saw

Yeah. Well. I'm not dumb. I don't lie, and I'm not one of those nuts, either. Ask anyone, anyone who's known me for the last twelve years, which is all the time I've been alive, if Ray Beane ever, I mean *ever* ran off at the mouth with stupid stuff nobody'd believe. I never did. I always tell it straight. My dad, before he died, that's the way he raised me. And my mom, she's the same way. *Be on the level with folks, Ray, and always look 'em in the eye.*

I live in Poma Valley, California. I was born here, like I said, twelve years ago, and I haven't hardly been anywhere else in all that time. Once, when I was nine—this was just before the Lord took my dad away with cancer—we went on a little trip south to San Francisco. It was just the three of us—my mom, my dad, and me—and we rode on the trolley car and saw some of the sights down there. But I guess that was about the only time I was out of Poma Valley. I have a grandpa from Ohio, but I have never visited him. He comes here sometimes to see us. See? I'm being as straight as I can be about everything, so nobody can say I lied or exaggerated or anything.

Poma Valley is a little town. Very rural, you'd call it. Only about five thousand people. And I go to school in a one-room schoolhouse, just like that old-fashioned program you see sometimes in reruns on TV. It's true. We have the sixth, seventh, and eighth grades all in one room. And there's only ten of us in all those classes. I get there by bus and it takes about forty-five minutes to an hour, depending on the roads and weather. Cross my heart. I know there are a lot of people who won't believe there are really places like that left in America, but there are, and I live in one. It's real, all right.

I know what's real.

I told you my name, but the whole of it is Raymond Earl Beane, Junior. I was named for my dad, and when I have a son of my own I'm going to name him Raymond Earle Beane the Third. My mom, she laughs and says I'd better have a wife who agrees with that choice, but I don't guess I'd marry somebody who didn't. Anyway, that's my name, and I said my age and mentioned everyone in my family except for some cousins who also live in Ohio, so that's it for my autobiography. We did autobiographies this year in seventh grade. Mine was pretty short.

I stand about five-two and weigh in at about one-hundred ten. I'm not very big but it doesn't bother me. I've got yellowish hair. It's straight and long, sort of, behind the ears. I like soccer and football and I like to listen to country music. Most of my friends like rock but I like country, and I don't care who knows it.

I have a dog. Maybe I should have mentioned him as part of my family, but I'll mention him now. He's part Lab and his name's Red. He's a black dog, but his name's Red and that's it.

I guess that's enough about me, but I wanted to tell the kind of person I am to help prove out what I say. Hope nobody minds.

The time I'm talking about now, it was six months ago in May. Just getting on to summer. What I wanted real bad was a team jacket. For soccer. I was on the team, and all the other kids had red jackets that said "Poma Valley Soccer" in white on the back with a picture of a soccer ball, and then you got your first name in white script writing put on the front on the left side. Boy, I wanted one, but we just couldn't afford it, Mom and me. See, I had a good jacket, so I didn't really need another one. This was just something I wanted. Around our house we can really just about deal with what we need. "Want" is something else.

So Mom said if I could raise the money over the summer, it'd be okay with her if I bought myself that jacket. And that's when it started.

Our main street, well, it's called Main Street and like you'd expect, it runs straight through town and then it turns into Route 34 and goes on to skirt by the farms. But there's a movie theater called the Poma on it, along with a pharmacy, a launderette, a Thom McAn shoe store, a hardware store, and a few other shops I can't remember. Oh, right, there's an army-navy store, too, and a diner on the corner. Out a ways in the other direction, there's an A&P and a bowling alley, too, and that's about it for Poma Valley.

The store I didn't mention is the little market between the launderette and the pharmacy. It sells groceries. It's called Meyer's.

I started out looking for work in the bowling alley. I wasn't sure what I could do, but I thought it would be fun to hang out there and maybe get to bowl a few frames every now and then, you know, improve my game. But no luck. So I moved on to the shoe store and the pharmacy (I skipped the launderette—doing the laundry at home is bad enough). I didn't have any luck there either and I finally ended up at Meyer's grocery store.

We never shopped at Meyer's. Mom says the little markets are always more expensive since they can't buy in bulk the way supermarkets can, so I had never met Mr. Meyer before. I guess I'd seen him some. I mean, you can't really miss anyone who lives in Poma Valley, but I never paid him any mind before that day. Funny thing was, he knew me.

"Ray Beane," he says when I come in. And he grins this big grin at me. I guess my jaw kind of drops and he laughs. His laugh is big and nice, not the kind of laugh where you think maybe he's making fun of you. "Sure I know you," he says. "I like to know who all the kids are."

I found out later that it was true he liked most of the kids, but he also wanted to keep an eye on us. There are plenty of kids who take stuff, rip it off, you know. And if he knew kids, called them by name and treated them nice, maybe they wouldn't do it so much to him. Take stuff, I mean.

He was a smart man, Mr. Meyer, but I didn't find any of this stuff out till later. Till I started working for him and getting to know him.

Yeah, he hired me. Minimum wage plus the tips I'd earn for deliveries. Part-time after school, and when school let out a few weeks later, full-time, ten till six. Sweep the place inside and out, dust the shelves, pack groceries, even wait on customers if he was busy, all the stuff you'd expect would be done in a small grocery store. What he didn't mention was he really wanted somebody to talk to. He talked a lot.

If that sounds as if I didn't like to hear him talk, then I said it wrong. I did like it.

Mr. Meyer's first name was Abe. Abraham. He was Jewish and spoke with an accent. He told me his age—sixty-seven. He was proud of it, he said, because he had been in a concentration camp[1] in the Second World War and any time he lived after that was "borrowed time." He laughed when he said it, but I knew he didn't think it was funny.

Except the thing is, he wasn't at all angry or anything, just grateful. He said he was grateful to have come out of such a dark and terrible time and be able to live in sunny California and run his own business, too.

He didn't have a family. He said they all died in the camp. He showed me two pictures, of a dark-haired woman and a little girl. The pictures were very old—they were black and white, and yellow around the edges, but he was proud of them and kept them in a gold frame in the back of the counter.

"My mother," he said. "And my sister." He told me their names,

1. **concentration camp:** place where the Nazis held, tortured, and killed Jewish people and others during World War II.

but I couldn't pronounce them. I know that the only time his eyes didn't laugh was when he looked at those two pictures.

The truth was that the store wasn't that busy most of the time. A lot of people must be like my mom and they shop at the A&P. Some folks'd come in for last-minute things like a newspaper or a carton of milk or bread or something, but not too much more. I may have made—tops—three deliveries all summer. But lunchtime was busy. Mr. Meyer made deli sandwiches, and the guys who worked on the roads and the truckers and local folks would come in for tuna salad, bologna, roast beef, whatever, and milk or a soda or beer. I guess that's where most of the money was made, the lunches. Anyway, he never complained about money, Mr. Meyer, so I guess he made enough for his needs. I didn't complain either, because so did I. And then some.

Except for lunchtime, we had time to kill, Mr. Meyer and me. We'd sit down behind the counter and he'd give me what he called his "philosophy of life."

"There's always someone worse off than you, Ray Beane," he'd say. He always called me Ray Beane, my whole name, like it was one word. "It's sad you have no papa, but a mama you have. There are boys who don't have both, you know. And not only that, your mama, she loves you very much, right?"

"Well, yeah . . ."

"Well, yeah, you say. Of course she loves you very much. To have someone to love you is a wonderful thing."

I wanted to ask him who he had to love *him*, except I thought it would be rude. Only he was one step ahead of me there.

"When I was young, I had a whole big family who loved me very much, so I know what it's like. Many people, they never know what it's like to be loved."

I looked at him.

"It's like the optimist and the pessimist, yes? The optimist has one glass of schnapps, he says it is half full. The pessimist has the same glass, he says it is half empty. You see the difference?"

I thought I did, except I didn't know what schnapps was.

"When you wake up in the morning, Ray Beane, what do you see?" he asked.

I thought for a second.

"Uh . . . my alarm clock . . . my closet door . . . Red, lots of times, he wakes me up."

"Do you see the sunlight streaming through your window?"

"Uh, yeah . . ."

"Uh, yeah. Does it make you feel good that another day is here? Another day when you can put on your clothes and your shoes and walk around, healthy, in the sunlight?"

"Uh, yeah . . ."

"Uh, yeah. Some vocabulary you got there, Ray Beane. We got to do something about that."

"I got an A in Vocabulary," I told him.

He smiled. "Only old men think about being lucky to wake up in the sunshine and walk around," he said. "Kids don't have to think about that. But it would be nice if they did. Just once in a while, Ray Beane. Think about it. It will make you a nicer person."

I didn't see how, but I liked him, so I decided to think about it. Once in a while.

"Did you know, Ray Beane, that ninety-nine percent of the things you worry about never, never happen?" he asked once.

"Huh?"

"It's true. Ninety-nine percent. A fact."

"Sometimes they do," I said.

"One percent. The odds are very good that worrying is a waste of time. And besides, worrying won't change what happens anyway, will it?"

I shook my head.

He shrugged this big shrug. His shoulders covered his ears. "So why worry?"

That was the kind of stuff he said, all the time. I told Mom about him and the things he said, and she said he sounded like a very wise man. She still doesn't shop there, though—she said everything in his place was at least a dime more than at the A&P.

Once my friend Frankie came in for candy. He was with his older brother and they were both acting wise. You know, kidding around, punching each other and ragging on us a little. Frankie was doing it because his brother Jim was there. Usually, he's pretty nice. But anyway, I saw Jim lift this Baby Ruth bar off the candy rack. I caught him in the big round magnifying mirror Mr. Meyer has at the front of the store, so you can see what's going on in the aisles. I didn't know what to do—I mean it. But still, there was Mr. Meyer and how nice he was to me and all—I mean, I always got to take stuff home at the end of the day and he was teaching me things—he made me learn a fact from the encyclopedia every single day and memorize it and tell it to him. He did.

I couldn't stand it. I turned red and my stomach hurt and then before I even knew it, Frankie and Jim were gone, outta there. My stomach hurt worse than before, but I still didn't say anything. And then I felt a hand on my shoulder.

"It's okay, Ray Beane. I knew they were your friends."

I felt like I was about to cry. Okay, I did cry.

"You're my friend too," I blubbered, feeling like a total wuss.

"A different kind," he said.

"Well, if you saw, how come you didn't say anything?" I asked, wiping my nose on my sleeve and feeling even stupider.

He didn't answer. I knew it was because he was waiting to see what I would do.

"I won't let it go again," I said, real softly.

"I won't put you in that position again," he said, even softer.

Later, after work, I found Frankie. I told him if he ever came in there with Jim again and ripped off Mr. Meyer, I'd personally break his face. I said *his*, not Jim's, because I couldn't take Jim. But I can take Frankie and he knows it, so it was a personal thing, between the two of us, and that way no one at school would have to know and Mr. Meyer wouldn't have to know and Frankie wouldn't let it happen again. I guessed. I hoped. I sort of worried about it every time Frankie came into the store with his brother, which wasn't that often, but neither of them even flicked a whisker, so Mr. Meyer was right about that—I worried for nothing.

It was what I *didn't* worry about that happened.

It was a Thursday. I know it was a Thursday. I woke up and thought about the sunshine that day. I was grinning all the way to work and I told Mr. Meyer about it and he grinned, too. And the day was bright and nice like it usually is, especially in summer. It was morning, before the lunch folks, so the store had its usual few customers. I remember Mrs. Lefton came in and bought cat food and Mrs. Crowley came in for orange juice and bread—she's the housekeeper for old Mr. Staley—and Willy Pelosi bought a paper, two doughnuts, and a black coffee. I remember all of that.

And I remember the truck. It was a red pickup and it pulled up right in front of the store, right there in the sunshine on Main Street, and one man jumped out of it. He was wearing a hat. And then it was fast and blurry and I don't like to talk about it, but this is the way it went.

The man had a gun and he pointed it right at us, Mr. Meyer and me. And he said he wanted money. He knew the old man kept a lot of it in a vault in the back and he wanted it, he wanted it. Mr. Meyer never said a word, but he was holding a can of bug spray—we were stacking them, the ant-and-roach-killer cans; he said they do pretty well in the summer—and suddenly he threw it, the can, he *threw* it right at the guy with the gun. He hit the guy and the guy dropped the gun, but not before it went off. And then Mr. Meyer, he picked up another spray can and sprayed the guy's face. The guy was yelling, because of the spray in his face, and I was so scared, I mean, I hope and pray never to be so scared again, but there was Mr. Meyer right next to me, saying, "It's okay, Ray Beane, get the gun, now before he can use it again, that's the boy, that's my boy, now hold it on him, I'm right here, we'll hold it on him, we'll do it together, just like we do things."

And he winked at me. He really did. Winked at me. I saw it.

Then I was holding the gun and hollering my head off. Outside I could hear the truck pulling away, grinding gears and blowing soot, and then Mr. Aiken from the pharmacy came in and he was with a whole bunch of people who heard the gun and the yelling and the truck and everything, and the police came and they took the gun away. He was still covering his face and crying or something from the spray in his eyes.

And then Mr. Aiken, he put his arm around my shoulders and he took me out of the store. Damned if I wasn't crying again, but I was shaking so bad I could hardly stand, I was still so scared.

"It's okay, Raymond. They've called your mom and she's on her way. It's all right, boy, it's all right," he kept saying.

And the crowd, I could hear the crowd. It was too early for the lunch folks, but they were there anyway—they just appeared, along with the rest of Poma Valley. I remember it all just perfectly, just like it was going on right this minute.

"Nothing like this *ever* happened before in the valley . . ."

"Did, too. Last year and the year before."

"That was the gas station got held up. And it was at night, no one was there."

"Was too there."

"Was not and there weren't no gun."

"One of 'em got away."

"Yeah, in a red pickup. They'll get him."

"Poor kid, poor Ray."

"Ray's the lucky one. Poor Meyer, that's who. Poor old guy."

That's when I stopped blubbering.

"What about Mr. Meyer?" I asked.

But instead of answering me, Mr. Aiken just kept patting and squeezing my shoulder. I moved quick then, and started to head back into the store, but Mr. Aiken and someone else grabbed me and held on to me and wouldn't let me go. So I *really* started hollering then, you bet, just yelling my fool head off for Mr. Meyer to come out. *"Come out! Mr. Meyer! Come out! Come out, Mr. Meyer!"*

But "Shh, boy" was all Mr. Aiken would say and everyone else just seemed to turn away from us, looking down at the sidewalk or up the street into the sun.

"He can't come out, Ray," Mrs. Lefton said. She took Mr. Aiken's place and pulled me away with her arm around my shoulder. "He can't come out, Ray, honey, he was shot. That shot everyone heard, it caught him, honey. You don't want to go back in there—"

But I did, and she couldn't hold me then. Nobody could. I raced past them, pushed past them. There wasn't anybody who could stop me then.

The paramedics from the volunteer ambulance corps were picking him up from where he'd been lying on the floor at the end of the shelf with all the bug sprays. They put him on a gurney,[2] and even though I knew he was dead, I still lost it when I saw them put the sheet over him.

They did catch the guy in the truck. His pal told them just where to find him. He also said how he heard "the old guy" had this safe in back of his store with all this money because Jews always have a lot of money they hoard, and how he knew the store was never busy that time of day, all kinds of stupid and weird stuff like that. I'm trying to

---

2. **gurney** [gėr′ nē]: stretcher or wheeled cot.

say how I remember it all and I do, anyone can see that, but it didn't come together for me until the police questioned me later. Actually, it was just Captain Ebsen, who sometimes takes my mother out, both of them being widowed. It was when he was asking me all those questions that everyone started looking at me funny.

See, the gun went off just once, and that's when Mr. Meyer had to have been shot. But it was *after* the gun went off that he sprayed the robber's face and told me to hold the gun on him and said we'd do it together, that he was with me. And winked at me.

But everyone said I was too upset to be rational. That's what they said. I wasn't rational, but it was understandable, they said, after what I went through.

Well, yeah, I guess I went through something. And I guess he'll always be with me, that old man and his old pictures and his "philosophy of life." And I don't guess I'll ever really get over what happened to him. I'll remember everything he said about being lucky and about worrying and about the sunshine and about the half-full glass, just like I know he'd want me to.

But after that shot went off, he was *there* next to me, calling me Ray Beane and telling me we'd do it together. And he winked at me.

I saw what I saw.

JUDIE ANGELL

Judie Angell was born in 1937 in New York City. She became an elementary school teacher before she began writing. She has said, "I think growing up heads the list of The Hardest Things to Do in Life. It's so hard, in fact, that some of us never get there." She tries, in her writing, to record memories, feelings, and imaginings in the hope that they will "help a little—make you laugh—make you feel you're not alone."

Angell is another user of pseudonyms. She has written for children under the name Maggie Twohill and as Fran Arrick for older readers. One of her novels for middle school readers (written as Judie Angell) is *Dear Lola, or How to Build Your Own Family.*

Asking Big Questions About the Literature

What does it mean to be a friend?

Theme

The main idea or message of a piece of literature is the **theme.** In this unit, one theme is *friends*. Think about how someone can be a friend. For example, in "The Chinese Checker Players," how can a six-year-old child and a ninety-three-year-old woman be friends? Are they friends simply because they play Chinese checkers? Choose two poems and write a paragraph to explain how each poem answers the question, "What does it mean to be a friend?" Before writing, use a cluster like the one shown to map out your ideas. (*See "Theme" on page 119.*)

PERFORM
a Conversation

With a partner, select two characters from one of the literature selections in this unit. Write the dialogue for a conversation these two characters might have about what it means to be a friend. Then perform the conversation for your class.

Define a Friend

In his book *How to Win Friends and Influence People*, Dale Carnegie says, "To make a friend, simply *be* one." Which character from the literature in this unit simply *is* a friend? Write a paragraph explaining why this character qualifies as a friend. Use examples from the literature to support your argument. Then display the quotation and your classmates' responses on a bulletin board.

What does it mean to have a friend?

Create a
SURVEY

With your classmates, develop a questionnaire about friendship and distribute it to students in your school. Collect the surveys, tabulate the results, and use them as the basis of a news article: "Teenagers' Views About Having Friends." Submit your article to the school newspaper.

LITERATURE STUDY
Character

A **character** is a person or animal who participates in the action of a work of literature. As a reader, you get to know literary characters in much the same way that you get to know new friends—by how they look, what they say, how they act, and what others think of them. Which of the characters in this unit would you most like to have as a friend? To help you sort out your ideas, first complete a chart like this one. Write about the character and why he or she would make a good friend. Then share your thoughts with a partner. (*See "Character" on page 118.*)

	Detail 1	Detail 2	Detail 3	Detail 4
Appearance				
Speech				
Behavior				
Opinion of others				

RANK *Characters*

Rank the characters in the selections that you've read on the basis of the quality of their friendship. Use a range of 1 through 5, with 1=good friend and 5=poor friend. Compare rankings with a partner, and explain how you arrived at your decisions.

Asking Big Questions About the Literature

What are different kinds of friendship?

TELEVISION TALK SHOW

In a small group, develop a script for a talk show that stars characters from different literature selections. Brainstorm questions and answers about how the characters met, how their relationships developed, and how they'd describe the friendship. After rehearsing, present your talk show to the class.

LITERATURE STUDY

Character

In literature, **characters** can be described as either round or flat. A *round* character is one whose personality is well-developed. A *flat* character, on the other hand, may have only one or two character traits. In your journal, brainstorm a list of the characters from this unit that you would define as round. Then choose two of them and explain in two or more paragraphs why you would classify each one as a round character. (*See "Character" on page 118.*)

EXAMINE Connotations and Denotations

While all words have exact definitions, or **denotations**, they also have **connotations**—those positive or negative feelings people associate with words. For example, two words like *friend* and *pal* may be alike in meaning, but each conveys a different connotation. In a small group, brainstorm synonyms for *friend*. Then make a chart showing the denotation and connotations for each word. Discuss how the connotations suggest different kinds of friendships.

Word	Denotation	Connotations
pal	person one knows, likes, and trusts	buddy, super best friend

How can friendships change?

LITERATURE STUDY

Theme

Writers often wish to convey their insights about the world and human nature. This central idea, or insight, about a subject is the **theme** of a work. Choose one of the literature selections you've read and rewrite it in a simplified form for children. Your purpose is to teach a lesson about how friendships change. Collect your classmates' stories in an anthology and share it with students in a local elementary school. (*See "Theme" on page 119.*)

Tell a Story

With a small group or in writing, tell a story about a change, for better or worse, that occurred in one of your friendships. Then discuss how the change you experienced is similar to one that occurred between two characters in a literature selection you've read.

Write a

SCENE

With a partner, choose one of the selections in this unit. Write a scene that might happen if two of the characters met again ten years later. Based on what you know about the characters, construct a time line to plot out what's happened to them. Then perform your scene for your class and lead a discussion about how and why the characters' relationship may have changed. For example, the time line on this page describes what may have happened to Ruri and Laurie in "The Bracelet."

Ruri leaves camp in Utah —moves to San Francisco.	Laurie goes to college in New York City.	Ruri visits cousins in New York City.
▼	▼	▼
3 years after story	5 years after story	8 years after story

NOW

Choose a Project!

Three projects involving friendship are described on the following pages. Which one is for you?

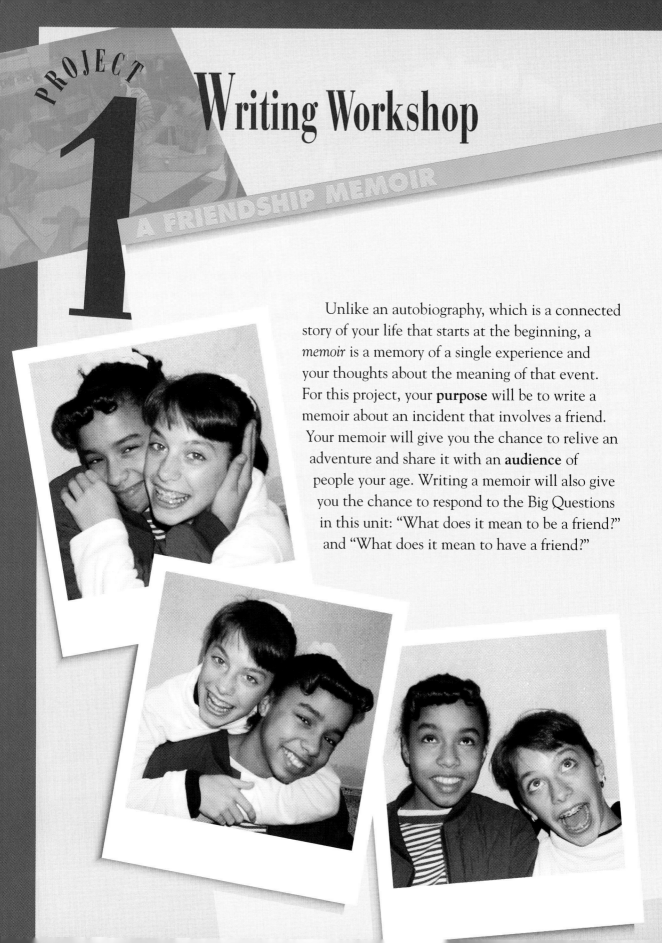

PROJECT 1

Writing Workshop

A FRIENDSHIP MEMOIR

Unlike an autobiography, which is a connected story of your life that starts at the beginning, a *memoir* is a memory of a single experience and your thoughts about the meaning of that event. For this project, your **purpose** will be to write a memoir about an incident that involves a friend. Your memoir will give you the chance to relive an adventure and share it with an **audience** of people your age. Writing a memoir will also give you the chance to respond to the Big Questions in this unit: "What does it mean to be a friend?" and "What does it mean to have a friend?"

Prewriting
CHOOSING AN INCIDENT

To help you recall incidents, try *clustering* your ideas by placing a friend's name in the center of a circle and branching your ideas out from there. Look at photo albums and school yearbooks to nudge your memory, or think of your life as a movie. Rerun possible scenes again and again until a picture emerges so vividly that it stops the reel. Whichever method you use, choose an incident that would interest an audience of your peers. What about the time you defended the underdog and won a friend—or the way a misunderstanding almost fractured the perfect friendship? Remember, an ordinary event can be as eye-opening and entertaining as a dramatic one.

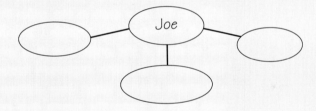

Prewriting
MAKING A PLAN

Writing a memoir is like going on a trip. If you don't know where you're going, you may never reach a destination. A map will help to guide your way. This map may be as simple as filling out a chart with headings for *purpose, conflict, setting, characters, dialogue,* and *resolution* (or *who, what, where, when, how,* and *why*).

Purpose	Conflict	Setting	Characters	Dialogue	Resolution

PROJECT 1 Writing Workshop

Drafting YOUR MEMOIR

Once you've chosen an incident to write about, selected an audience, and mapped out ideas, you're ready to write your first draft. The following guidelines will help you draft your memoir.

Guidelines for Drafting a Memoir

Use the **first-person point of view** and the personal pronoun *I*. For example, Jennifer Haynes, a student writer, uses first-person pronouns to tell about a fishing experience on pages 110-111.

- Experiment with different kinds of introductions, such as providing background information, establishing the setting, introducing the characters through dialogue, or arousing curiosity with a question as Jennifer does in her introduction.

- The simplest way to write a memoir is to use **chronological order** to tell your story in the order that the events happened. In "Fishing for Friends," Jennifer relates the events of the incident in the order that they occurred. Some writers use **flashback** to establish important background information. For a dramatic impact, begin your memoir with the ending, then flash back to reveal the events that led up to it.

- Introduce **setting** early in your memoir. Use descriptive details or reveal the setting gradually through the action.

- Keep in mind the ways in which writers accomplish **characterization**. Make your characters believable.

- Remember that everyone has a unique way of talking. As you write the characters' **dialogue**, keep in mind that people ramble, interrupt each other, or stop abruptly. Read the dialogue aloud to yourself or to a partner to see if it sounds natural.

- Write a **conclusion** that will express what the incident meant to you. Jennifer closes her memoir with a comment about her teacher, who is the central figure in her writing.

- Write a **title** that attracts your readers' attention and arouses their curiosity. Make sure that the title suggests what your memoir is about. For example, Jennifer's title, "Fishing for Friends," arouses curiosity and suggests a fishing incident.

Revising YOUR MEMOIR

As you read what you've written, ask yourself whether you've fulfilled your purpose. Have you expressed your feelings about a particular friendship? Does every detail, sentence, and paragraph clearly express what you want to say?

Look for ways of bringing your memoir to life. Would more dialogue move the action along and emphasize the conflict? Would adding more detail increase the suspense? If you get stuck at any point, go back to your prewriting notes.

You may want to test your memoir at this point by reading it aloud to a group of classmates. Their questions and reactions may pinpoint other areas that you need to work on. For example, if your classmates are confused about what happens when, you may need to add details or transitions to make the order of events clearer.

Editing YOUR MEMOIR

After you've revised your memoir, exchange your work with a partner or other writing group members. Read and edit each other's work. Look carefully for errors in grammar, usage, spelling, and punctuation. Then correct the errors that have been pointed out. Pay special attention to punctuating and paragraphing dialogue correctly.

Publishing YOUR MEMOIR

Once you've completed your memoir, you can share it with your classmates in a number of ways.

- Present it as a gift to the friend who is featured in it.
- Submit it to your school's literary magazine or to one of the national student writing publications.
- Turn it into a screenplay that you and several classmates can videotape.
- Publish a class anthology of memoirs and accompanying photographs that could be donated to the school or community library.

Fishing For Friends

a memoir by Jennifer Haynes, West Palm Beach, Florida

It was the first day of my summer vacation and where do you think I ended up? That's right—back at school! I had made a deal with my teacher, so there I was at 10:30 A.M. with my friend Tammi back in Mr. Tufts' classroom. The classroom was just as cluttered as we had left it the day before. The books were stacked a mile high ready to be packed away, and the posters were practically leaning off the walls screaming for our attention. When we entered the classroom, Mr. Tufts, my English teacher (some people call him Mr. T), was sitting at his desk.

"Hi! We're here," I said, as we leaned our fishing poles against the bulletin board. He didn't have to say a word. We knew our job and we knew our deal. Nonetheless, his military salute commanded us into action.

"Great! Right on time! Let's get busy. Take down the posters, pack the books, and pick up any papers on the floor. When you're done, we can post the sign: Gone Fishing!"

It was after lunch when Tammi and I finished the tasks. The once cluttered room looked quite empty now. Seeing that we had completed our part of the deal, Mr. Tufts herded us out of the classroom and posted his sign. "Now for my part of the deal," he said. "Pizza and fish!"

Tammi laughed and said, "Mr. Tufts, I do hope you don't mean we're going to use the fish we catch as topping for the pizza!"

Jokingly he replied, "Well, you'll have to wait and see!"

His response reminded me of how he would bait us like that and memories of a fun year flashed through my mind. As we walked toward the exit sign, I stopped myself just in time from tripping over Tammi's pole. Trying to hide my embarrassment, I just laughed with them.

When we reached the parking lot, Mr. Tufts' blue truck was not there! He had forgotten that his son had left him off at school and had borrowed the truck for the day. "So much for our fishing plans!" I thought. But luckily, we found a ride from another teacher, who pretended not to mind having our fishing poles hang out of her car window.

When we pulled up to Mr. Tufts' waterfront home, Tammi shyly asked, "Uh, Mr. T, would it be all right if I invited my friend, Mike, who lives nearby, to fish with us?"

"Sure," he said, "as long as he can catch a fish for pizza topping!" In an instant, Tammi was on the phone to Mike. Her invitation not only hooked Mike but also Adam!

After fishing unsuccessfully in front of Mr. T's place, we moved to the waterfront by Adam's grandparents' house. There our luck changed and all of us caught many fish. However, we didn't keep any of them. We simply threw the slimy things back into the water. I think deep down I just wanted to make sure we didn't have any to use as pizza topping—just in case Mr. T wasn't kidding!

By 6:30, the second part of Mr. T's promise came true. The pizza arrived. Leaving all fish behind, we went back to his deck and devoured our meal. It was delicious!

"We should do this again," I suggested.

"Maybe in another week," Mike blurted out.

That day I made two new friends, Mike and Adam, all because I helped my teacher clean up our classroom.

The day ended when my Mom picked up Tammi and me at Mr. T's home. It was a nice way to end my year as a seventh grader. I certainly have some great memories—thanks to a teacher who cared enough to take us fishing!

Cooperative Learning

ADVERTISING A FRIENDSHIP WEEK

Do particular television commercials stand out in your memory? How about magazine or newspaper advertisements? Can you think of other ways people sell products? With this project, you'll have the opportunity to develop and sell an idea called Friendship Week. First, you'll work with your class to list events for the week. Then you'll work in small groups to develop ways to advertise the events. Your end product will be an advertising campaign to let people know about Friendship Week.

The PROCESS

Imagine that you and your classmates are the producers of a local television network and you plan to sponsor a Friendship Week. The agenda for the week includes special television programs focusing on the importance of friendship. With your classmates, brainstorm a list of programs and activities on the chalkboard. Once you've agreed on your agenda, change roles and imagine that you're part of an advertising agency.

To be part of an advertising agency, you and your classmates will form small groups—each representing a different agency. First, decide on a name for your agency. Then decide how your advertising team will publicize Friendship Week for the local television network. Use the following three assignments to structure your ideas.

1. Make a poster.
2. Write and design a brochure.
3. Write and perform a commercial.

Now decide how your group will complete its assignments. Depending on the size of your group, you may divide the tasks, or all of you may need to work on the tasks together. Whatever your approach, make a chart like the one below to help you keep track of who will do what, what materials you need, and how much time will be allowed to complete each task.

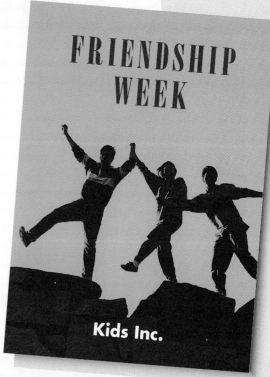

FRIENDSHIP WEEK

Kids Inc.

Tasks	Materials	Due Date	Person Responsible

The PRESENTATION

As a class, decide on a time and place for the presentations of the advertising campaigns for Friendship Week. Remember each group should display a poster, pass out a brochure (make copies if possible), and perform a commercial.

After each presentation, display the brochures and posters in the classroom. Then have a class discussion about the variety of ideas presented by each advertising agency.

Helping Your Community

A FRIEND-TO-MY-COMMUNITY DAY

One of the Big Questions in this unit asks, "What are different kinds of friendship?" In this project, you'll explore this question as you and your classmates develop and propose a plan for making community improvements during a Friend-to-My-Community Day.

Choosing A PLAN

With a partner or a small group, begin by brainstorming a list of ways you can be a friend to your community. Perhaps you know of an unsightly vacant lot that would make a wonderful community garden, or a neighborhood school that could use a litter patrol. Complete the statement below with one of the ideas from your brainstorming list.

• I'll become a friend to my community by_____.

Then develop your plan by using the following guidelines.

Laying THE GROUNDWORK

Depending on the community project you select, you may need permission and cooperation. For example, a *create-a-garden* plan may need the approval of the local authorities and the help of a garden club. To enlist the help of others, decide whether to write letters or to make a personal visit.

Developing YOUR PLAN

Now that you've thought out what you want to do and how to do it, it's time to develop and write your plan. Begin by explaining your purpose for having a Friend-to-My-Community Day.

Organizing YOUR TASKS

Next form committees that will show volunteers what needs to be done. For example, you might set up separate committees for Publicity, Materials, and Donations. Make a list like the following one to organize your tasks and provide a deadline to indicate when the tasks should be completed.

Publicity Committee			
Person	Task	Materials	Due Date
Maria	Poster	Posterboard markers	2/16
John	Poster		
Sarah			
Jesse			

Launching YOUR PLAN

Use charts to present your plan. Be sure to include the details you've defined in the previous steps. Then present your plan for a Friend-to-My-Community Day to the class.

If it's not possible for your class to carry out the plan, send your plan to some organization that can make it a reality—the town council or a local charity. You too can make a difference.

Putting It All Together

How Have Your Ideas About Friendship Changed?

After meeting the characters in this unit, how have your ideas about friendship changed? Review the writing you did earlier in the unit, such as your journal responses to the Big Questions and your Writing Workshop. Has the meaning of friendship changed for you? With your classmates, share and discuss your thoughts on this topic. Then compose an essay or a poem that explains your definition of friendship.

CHANGING IDEAS ABOUT FRIENDSHIP

Prewriting and Drafting   To help you generate ideas for your essay or poem, think about the following questions. Which character from this unit best reflects your feelings about friendship? How would you define friendship? What are the qualities of true friendship? Don't forget to consider the poetry selections when you think about the literature in this unit.

Now draft an essay or poem that explains your definition of friendship. In your writing, explain how your perspective on friendship has broadened. Be sure to support your definition with specific references to the literature. Include two or more characters, incidents, or even quotations from the literature. You may even want to add examples from your own life.

Revising and Editing   First, review your own writing by reading it aloud to yourself. Make sure that you have expressed your main idea clearly, supported it with examples, and used vivid, colorful words. Next exchange papers with a classmate to check grammar, punctuation, and spelling. Then make any appropriate corrections.

Publishing   If you choose to share your essay with the whole class, you should now decide how the class's essays and poems should be organized. Then extend your creativity and design a cover for a collection of your classmates' writing called *Reflections on Friendship*. Share your collection with another class or display it in your school library.

Evaluating Your Work

Think Back About the Big Questions

With a partner, discuss the Big Questions on pages 10 and 11 and revisit the ideas you listed in your journal for *Now Think* on page 11. Compare your current ideas about friendship with your thoughts at the beginning of this unit.

Think Back About Your Work

Now that you've completed this unit, it's time to think about and evaluate your work. Think back about your journal responses, writing activities, and projects. Then, in a letter to a real or imaginary friend, try to capture what you have accomplished in this unit. Use the following questions to help you write your letter.

- Which literature selections changed your ideas about friendship?

- Which literature selections were most interesting? Least interesting? Why?

- What were your favorite and least favorite activities? Why?

- What did you learn as you worked on your project?

- What would you do differently if you worked on a similar project again?

- How would you rate your work in this unit? Use the following scale and explain why and how you chose this number.

1 = Outstanding	3 = Fair
2 = Good	4 = Not as good as it could have been

CHARACTER

What Is Character?

Character is the term for a person or animal that participates in the action of a work of literature. The characters in a work of literature can be divided into two categories: *main characters* and *minor characters*. *Main characters* are those people or animals that are the most important characters in a work of literature. For example, in the story "I Saw What I Saw," the main characters are the narrator, Ray Beane, and the grocer, Mr. Meyer. The *minor characters* are those who are not central to the action in a story. For example, in the story "I Saw What I Saw," some of the minor characters are Ray's mother, Frankie, Mr. Aiken, and the gunman.

Developing a Character

Make a list of the characters found in one of the literature selections that you've read in this unit. Then label each character as either *main* or *minor*. If you could develop one of the minor characters into a main character, which one would you choose? What changes would you make to this character, and how would these changes affect the outcome of the story? In a paragraph or two, explain the change or changes you would make to this minor character. Be sure to show how the outcome of the story would be affected. Share your writing with your classmates by creating a bulletin–board display with the title "Developing Characters."

Extending Your Vocabulary

What does the word *character* really mean? Sometimes you may hear, "Oh, what a *character* he is!" "Is she one of the *characters* in this production?" Obviously, there are many ways to use the word *character*. Look up in a dictionary the meanings listed for *character* and select three of them. Then write a paragraph explaining the meanings you have selected. Be sure to provide sentence examples, like the ones above, for each meaning you choose for the word *character*. Compare your selections with a partner.

What Is Theme?

Theme is the main idea of a work of literature. It is the underlying message, which a writer most often implies rather than states. For example, the short story that ends this unit, "I Saw What I Saw," is about an adolescent who gets a job in a small grocery store in order to earn some extra money. Yet underlying that is the theme that friendship can grow in the most surprising places. We see this in the bond that develops between Ray and Mr. Meyer, the grocery store owner. To help you fully understand the theme of a literary work, focus on two aspects of the selection. First, ask yourself in what ways the main character has changed. Then ask how the conflict in the story has been settled. The answers should give you a better understanding of the theme.

Writing to the Editor Suppose that the publishers of this unit contacted you about helping them with a revision of this book. Write a letter to the editor about which selections you would keep and explain why. Also suggest ideas you have for replacements. Make sure that your replacements fit in with the *theme* of this unit. Then design a book jacket with information about the book itself. Use your letters and book jackets for a bulletin-board display.

Creating a Theme Park Have you ever been to a theme park? In case you haven't, it's a park filled with amusement rides related to a theme. If the park were called "Storyland Park," the names of the rides would be linked to children's stories—for example, a roller coaster might be called the "Mad Hatter." With a partner or small group, brainstorm a list of ideas for a *Friendship Theme Park*. Think of some friendship stories, like *The Incredible Journey*, or some from this unit like "The Bracelet" for ideas. Then map out the park and label all the sections. Present your plan to your class.

GLOSSARY OF LITERARY TERMS

A

alliteration   Repetition of the first sound—usually a consonant sound—in several words of a sentence or a line of poetry.

allusion   An author's indirect reference to someone or something that is presumed to be familiar to the reader.

anecdote   A short narrative about an interesting or humorous event, usually in the life of a person.

antagonist   The person or force opposing the protagonist or main character in a literary work. [See also *protagonist*.]

autobiography   A person's written account of his or her own life.

B

ballad   A poem, often a song, that tells a story in simple verse.

biography   An account of a person's life, written by another person.

blank verse   Unrhymed poetry.

C

character   A person or an animal that participates in the action of a work of literature. A *dynamic character* is one whose thoughts, feelings, and actions are changeable and lifelike; a *static character* always remains the same. [See also *protagonist, antagonist.*]

characterization   The creation of characters through the characters' use of language and through descriptions of their appearance, thoughts, emotions, and actions. [See also *character.*]

chronology   An arrangement of events in the order in which they happen.

cliché   An overused expression that sounds trite rather than meaningful.

climax   The highest point of tension in the plot of a work of literature. [See also *plot*.]

comedy   An amusing play that has a happy ending.

conclusion   The final part or ending of a piece of literature.

concrete poem   A poem arranged on the page so that its punctuation, letters, and lines make the shape of the subject of the poem.

conflict   A problem that confronts the characters in a piece of literature. The conflict may be *internal* (a character's struggle within himself or herself) or *external* (a character's struggle against nature, another person, or society). [See also *plot*.]

context   The general sense of words that helps readers to understand the meaning of unfamiliar words and phrases in a piece of writing.

D

description   An author's use of words to give the reader or listener a mental picture, impression, or understanding of a person, place, thing, event, or idea.

dialect   A form of speech spoken by people in a particular group or geographical region that differs in vocabulary, grammar, and pronunciation from the standard language.

dialogue   The spoken words and conversation of characters in a work of literature.

drama   A play that is performed before an audience according to stage directions and using dialogue. Classical drama has two genres: *tragedy* and *comedy*. Modern drama includes *melodrama, satire, theater of the absurd,* and *pantomime.* [See also *comedy, play,* and *tragedy.*]

dramatic poetry   A play written in the form of poetry.

E

epic   A long narrative poem written in a formal style and meant to be read aloud that relates the adventures and experiences of one or more great heroes or heroines.

essay   Personal nonfiction writing about a particular subject that is important to the writer.

excerpt   A passage from a larger work that has been taken out of its context to be used for a special purpose.

exposition   Writing that explains, analyzes, or defines.

extended metaphor   An elaborately drawn out metaphor. [See also *metaphor*.]

F

fable   A short, simple story whose purpose is to teach a lesson, usually with animal characters who talk and act like people.

fantasy   Imaginative fiction about unrealistic characters, places, and events.

fiction   Literature, including the short story and the novel, that tells about imaginary people and events.

figurative language Language used to express ideas through figures of speech: descriptions that aren't meant to be taken literally. Types of figurative language include *simile, metaphor, extended metaphor, hyperbole*, and *personification*.

figure of speech   A type of figurative language, not meant to be taken literally, that expresses something in such a way that it brings the thing to life in the reader's or listener's imagination. [See also *figurative language*.]

flashback   A break in a story's action that relates a past happening in order to give the reader background information about a present action in the story.

folktale   A story that has been passed along from storyteller to storyteller for generations. Kinds of folktales include *tall tales, fairy tales, fables, legends*, and *myths*.

foreshadowing   The use of clues to create suspense by giving the reader or audience hints of events to come.

free verse   Poetry that has no formal rhyme scheme or metrical pattern.

G

genre   A major category of art. The three major literary genres are poetry, prose, and drama.

H

haiku   A three-line Japanese verse form. In most haiku, the first and third lines have five syllables, while the second line has seven. The traditional haiku describes a complicated feeling or thought in simple language through a single image.

hero/heroine   The main character in a work of literature. In heroic literature, the hero or heroine is a particularly brave, noble, or clever person whose achievements are unusual and important. [See also *character*.]

heroic age   The historical period in western civilization—from about 800 B.C. through A.D. 200—during which most works of heroic literature, such as myths and epics, were created in ancient Greece and Rome.

hubris   Arrogance or excessive pride leading to mistakes; the character flaw in a hero of classical tragedy.

hyperbole   An obvious exaggeration used for emphasis. [See also *figurative language*.]

I

idiom   An expression whose meaning cannot be understood from the ordinary meaning of the words. For example, *It's raining cats and dogs*.

imagery   The words and phrases in writing that appeal to the senses of sight, hearing, taste, touch, and smell.

irony   An effect created by a sharp contrast between what is expected and what is real. An *ironic twist* in a plot is an event that is the complete opposite of what the characters have been hoping or expecting will happen. An *ironic statement* declares the opposite of the speaker's literal meaning.

J

jargon   Words and phrases used by a group of people who share the same profession or special interests in order to refer to technical things or processes with which they are familiar. In general, jargon is any terminology that sounds unclear, overused, or pretentious.

L

legend   A famous folktale about heroic actions, passed along by word of mouth from generation to generation. The legend may have begun as a factual account of real people and events but has become mostly or completely fictitious.

limerick   A form of light verse, or humorous poetry, written in one five-line stanza with a regular scheme of rhyme and meter.

literature   The branch of art that is expressed in written language and includes all written genres.

lyric poem   A short poem that expresses personal feelings and thoughts in a musical way. Originally, lyrics were the words of songs that were sung to music played on the lyre, a stringed instrument invented by the ancient Greeks.

M

metamorphosis   The transformation of one thing, or being, into another completely different thing or being, such as a caterpillar's change into a butterfly.

metaphor   Figurative language in which one thing is said to be another thing. [See also *figurative language*.]

meter   The pattern of rhythm in lines of poetry. The most common meter, in poetry written in English, is iambic pentameter, that is, a verse having five metrical feet, each foot of verse having two syllables, an unaccented one followed by an accented one.

mood   The feeling or atmosphere that a reader senses while reading or listening to a work of literature.

motivation   A character's reasons for doing, thinking, feeling, or saying something. Sometimes an author will make a character's motivation obvious from the beginning. In realistic fiction and drama, however, a character's motivation may be so complicated that the reader discovers it gradually, by studying the character's thoughts, feelings, and behavior.

myth   A story, passed along by word of mouth for generations, about the actions of gods and goddesses or super-human heroes and heroines. Most myths were first told to explain the origins of natural things or to justify the social rules and customs of a particular society.

N

narration   The process of telling a story. For both fiction and nonfiction, there are two main kinds of narration, based on whether the story is told from first-person or third-person point of view. [See also *point of view*.]

narrative poem   A poem that tells a story containing the basic literary ingredients of fiction: character, setting, and plot.

narrator   The person, or voice, that tells a story. [See also *point of view*, *voice*.]

nonfiction   Prose that is factually true and is about real people, events, and places.

nonstandard English Versions of English, such as slang and dialects, that use pronunciation, vocabulary, idiomatic expressions, grammar, and punctuation that differ from the accepted "correct" constructions of English.

novel A long work of narrative prose fiction. A novel contains narration, a setting or settings, characters, dialogue, and a more complicated plot than a short story.

O

oral tradition Stories, poems, and songs that have been kept alive by being told, recited, and sung by people over many generations. Since the works were not originally written, they often have many different versions.

onomatopoeia The technique of using words that imitate the sounds they describe, such as *hiss*, *buzz*, and *splash*.

P

parable A brief story, similar to a fable, but about people, that describes an ordinary situation and concludes with a short moral or lesson to be learned.

personification Figurative language in which an animal, an object, or an idea is given human characteristics. [See also *figurative language*.]

persuasion A type of speech or writing whose purpose is to convince people that something is true or important.

play A work of dramatic literature written for performance by actors before an audience. In classical or traditional drama, a play is divided into five acts, each containing a number of scenes. Each act represents a distinct phase in the development of the plot. Modern plays often have only one act and one scene.

playwright The author of a play.

plot The sequence of actions and events in fiction or drama. A traditional plot has at least three parts: the *rising action*, leading up to a turning point that affects the main character; the *climax*, the turning point or moment of greatest intensity or interest; and the *falling action*, leading away from the conflict, or resolving it.

poetry Language selected and arranged in order to say something in a compressed or nonliteral way. Modern poetry may or may not use many of the traditional poetic techniques that include *meter*, *rhyme*, *alliteration*, *figurative language*, *symbolism*, and *specific verse forms*.

point of view The perspective from which a writer tells a story. *First-person* narrators tell the story from their own point of view, using pronouns like *I* or *me*. *Third-person* narrators, using pronouns like *he*, *she*, or *them*, may be *omniscient* (knowing everything about all characters), or *limited* (taking the point of view of one character). [See also *narration*.]

propaganda Information or ideas that may or may not be true, but are spread as though they are true, in order to persuade people to do or believe something.

prose The ordinary form of written and spoken language used to create fiction, nonfiction, and most drama.

protagonist The main character of a literary work. [See also *character* and *characterization*.]

R

refrain A line or group of lines that is repeated, usually at the end of each verse, in a poem or a song.

repetition The use of the same formal element more than once in a literary work, for emphasis or in order to achieve another desired effect.

resolution The "falling action" in fiction or drama,

including all of the developments that follow the climax and show that the story's conflict is over. [See also *plot*.]

rhyme scheme   A repeated pattern of similar sounds, usually found at the ends of lines of poetry or poetic drama.

rhythm   In poetry, the measured recurrence of accented and unaccented syllables in a particular pattern. [See also *meter*.]

S

scene   The time, place, and circumstances of a play or a story. In a play, a scene is a section of an act. [See also *play*.]

science fiction   Fantasy literature set in an imaginary future, with details and situations that are designed to seem scientifically possible.

setting   The time and place of a work of literature.

short story   Narrative prose fiction that is shorter and has a less complicated plot than a novel. A short story contains narration, at least one setting, at least one character, and usually some dialogue.

simile   Figurative language that compares two unlike things, introduced by the words "like" or "as." [See also *figurative language*.]

soliloquy   In a play, a short speech spoken by a single character when he or she is alone on the stage. A soliloquy usually expresses the character's innermost thoughts and feelings, when he or she thinks no other characters can hear.

sonnet   A poem written in one stanza, using fourteen lines of iambic pentameter. [See also *meter*.]

speaker   In poetry, the individual whose voice seems to be speaking the lines. [See also *narration*, *voice*.]

stage directions   The directions, written by the playwright, to tell the director, actors, and theater technicians how a play should be dramatized. Stage directions may specify such things as how the setting should appear in each scene, how the actors should deliver their lines, when the stage curtain should rise and fall, how stage lights should be used, where on the stage the actors should be during the action, and when sound effects should be used.

stanza   A group of lines in poetry set apart by blank lines before and after the group; a poetic verse.

style   The distinctive way in which an author composes a

work of literature in written or spoken language.

suspense   An effect created by authors of various types of fiction and drama, especially adventure and mystery plots, to heighten interest in the story.

symbol   An image, person, place, or thing that is used to express the idea of something else.

T

tall tale   A kind of folk tale, or legend, that exaggerates the characteristics of its hero or heroine.

theme   The main idea or underlying subject of a work of literature.

tone   The attitude that a work of literature expresses to the reader through its style.

tragedy   In classical drama, a tragedy depicts a noble hero or heroine who makes a mistake of judgment that has disastrous consequences.

verse   A stanza in a poem. Also, a synonym for poetry as a genre. [See also *stanza*.]

voice   The narrator or the person who relates the action of a piece of literature. [See also *speaker*.]

ACKNOWLEDGMENTS

Grateful acknowledgment is made for permission to reprint the following copyrighted material.

"The Bracelet" by Yoshiko Uchida is reprinted by permission of the Estate of Yoshiko Uchida.

"A bald display of solidarity" is reprinted from *The Boston Globe*, December 5, 1992 by permission of the Associated Press.

"Our Good Day" from *The House on Mango Street* by Sandra Cisneros. Copyright © 1989 by Sandra Cisneros. Published in the United States by Vintage Books, a division of Random House, Inc., New York, and distributed in Canada by Random House of Canada Limited, Toronto. Originally published, in somewhat different form, by Arte Público Press in 1984 and revised in 1989. Reprinted by permission of Susan Bergholz Literary Services, New York.

"The Squirrel's Loan" by Partap Sharma is reprinted from *The Surangini Tales* by Partap Sharma published by Harcourt Brace Jovanovich, 1973. Permission granted by the author.

"Telephone Talk" by X. J. Kennedy. Reprinted with permission of Margaret L. McElderry Books, an imprint of Macmillan Publishing Company from *The Kite That Braved Old Orchard Beach* by X. J. Kennedy. Copyright © 1991 by X. J. Kennedy.

"A Time to Talk" by Robert Frost from *The Poetry of Robert Frost* edited by Edward Connery Lathem. Copyright 1944 by Robert Frost. Copyright 1916, © 1969 by Henry Holt and Company, Inc. Reprinted by permission of Henry Holt and Company, Inc.

"The Osage Orange Tree" by William Stafford is reprinted by permission of the author.

"Where Are You Now, William Shakespeare?" by M. E. Kerr from *Me Me Me Me Me,* copyright © 1983 by M. E. Kerr, a Charlotte Zolotow book. Reprinted by permission of HarperCollins Publisher.

"Thank You, M'am" by Langston Hughes from *The Langston Hughes Reader,* copyright © 1958 by Langston Hughes. Reprinted by permission of the Harold Ober Agency.

"Amigo Brothers" by Piri Thomas from *Stories From El Barrio.* Copyright © 1978 by Piri Thomas. Reprinted by permission of Alfred A. Knopf, Inc.

"Hannah Armstrong" by Edgar Lee Masters from *Spoon River Anthology* by Edgar Lee Masters, originally published by the Macmillan Co. Permission by Ellen C. Masters.

"Graduates hear some Clinton advice" from *The Boston Globe,* May 17, 1993 is reprinted by permission of the Associated Press.

"Lob's Girl" by Joan Aiken from *A Whisper in the Night,* copyright © 1981, 1982, 1983, 1984 by Joan Aiken Enterprises, Ltd. Reprinted by permission of Dell Publishing, a division of The Bantam Doubleday Dell Publishing Group, Inc.

"The Chinese Checker Players" by Richard Brautigan from *The Pill versus The Springhill Mine Disaster,* copyright © 1968 by Richard Brautigan is reproduced by permission of the Helen Brann Agency.

"Mr. Misenheimer's Garden" from *On The Road With Charles Kuralt* by Charles Kuralt. Reprinted by permission of The Putnam Publishing Group. Copyright © 1985 by CBS, Inc.

"I Saw What I Saw" by Judie Angell, copyright © 1992 by Judie Angell, from *Within Reach,* edited by Donald Gallo, copyright © 1993. By permission of HarperCollins Publisher.

ILLUSTRATION

26-27 Jennifer Hewitson; 32-37 Karen Watson; 40-47 R.J. Shay.

PHOTOGRAPHY

4 *l* Julie Bidwell/©D.C. Heath; *r* Skjold/The Image Works; 5 Courtesy Estate of Romare Bearden. Collection of Dr. and Mrs. Cyril J. Jones; 6 Sarah Putnam/©D.C. Heath; 8 Stephen Simpson/FPG International; 9 Erika Stone; 10 *t* Mary Kate Denny/PhotoEdit; *b* John Owens/©D.C. Heath; 11 *t* Mary Kate Denny/PhotoEdit; *b* Jim Whitmer/Stock Boston; 12, 15, 16, 17 Mine Okubo; 19 Photo by Deborah Storm/Courtesy of Macmillan Children's Book Group; 20-21 Karen Kerckhove; 23-24 National Museum of Modern Art, Paris/SCALA/Art Resource, NY. ©1995 ARS, NY/ADAGP, Paris; 25 AP/Wide World Photos; 28 Roy Lichtenstein. Courtesy of James Goodman Gallery, New York; 29 Dorothy M. Kennedy; 30 UPI/The Bettmann Archive; 30-31 Boston Public Library Print Department; 47 Photo by Zoe Kamitses; 48 The Howard University Gallery of Art, Permanent Collection, Washington, D.C.; 51 Courtesy Estate of Romare Bearden; 53 UPI/The Bettmann Archive; 54 Private Collection, California; 65 Alex Gotfrey; 66-67 *background* Peter Gridley/FPG International; 67 *t* Gift of Mr. and Mrs. William H. Lane and the Hayden Collection, by exchange. Courtesy, Museum of Fine Arts, Boston. 1990.376; *b* UPI/The Bettmann Archive; 68 Joe Sohn/Chromosohn/The Stock Market; 70-71 Karen Kasmauski/Woodfin Camp; 76 Adam Woolfitt/Woodfin Camp; 83 Photo by Rod Delroy. Courtesy of St. Martin's Press; 84-85 Louis K. Meisel Gallery, New York; 86-87, 88-89 Craig Hammell/The Stock Market; 89 CBS News; 90-91 Steve Proehl/The Image Bank; 94-95 David Hamilton/The Image Bank; 98 Susan Leavines/Photo Researchers; 101 Courtesy of Macmillan Children's Goup; 103 Nancy Sheehan/©D.C. Heath; 106 *t* Elizabeth Hamlin/Stock Boston; *b* Shawna Johnston; 110 Peter Fronk/Tony Stone Images; 112 Jean-Claude Lejeune/Stock Boston; 113 Nancy Sheehan/The Picture Cube; 114 *t* J. Sulley/The Image Works; 114 *b*-115 Courtesy of Wasatch Fish & Gardens, Salt Lake City, UT. **Back cover** *t* Julie Bidwell/©D.C. Heath; *c* Sarah Putnam/©D.C. Heath; *b* John Owens/©D.C. Heath.

Full Pronunciation Key for Footnoted Words

(Each pronunciation and definition is adapted from *Scott, Foresman Advanced Dictionary* by E.L. Thorndike and Clarence L. Barnhart.)

The pronunciation of each footnoted word is shown just after the word, in this way: **abbreviate** [ə brē′ vē āt]. The letters and signs used are pronounced as in the words below. The mark ′ is placed after a syllable with primary or heavy accent, as in the example above. The mark ′ after a syllable shows a secondary or lighter accent, as in **abbreviation** [ə brē′ vē ā′ shən].

Some words, taken from foreign languages, are spoken with sounds that do not otherwise occur in English. Symbols for these sounds are given in the key as "foreign sounds."

a	hat, cap	j	jam, enjoy	u	cup, butter	**foreign sounds**
ā	age, face	k	kind, seek	u̇	full, put	
ä	father, far	l	land, coal	ü	rule, move	Y as in French *du*.
		m	me, am	v	very, save	Pronounce (ē) with
b	bad, rob	n	no, in	w	will, woman	the lips rounded as
ch	child, much	ng	long, bring	y	young, yet	for (ü).
d	did, red			z	zero, breeze	
		o	hot, rock	zh	measure, seizure	à as in French *ami*.
e	let, best	ō	open, go			Pronounce (ä) with
ē	equal, be	ô	order, all	ə represents:		the lips spread and
ėr	term, learn	oi	oil, voice		a in about	held tense.
		ou	house, out		e in taken	
f	fat, if				i in pencil	œ as in French *peu*.
g	go, bag	p	paper, cup		o in lemon	Pronounce (ā) with the
h	he, how	r	run, try		u in circus	lips rounded as for (ō).
		s	say, yes			
i	it, pin	sh	she, rush			N as in French *bon*.
ī	ice, five	t	tell, it			The N is not pro-
		th	thin, both			nounced, but shows
		ŦH	then, smooth			that the vowel before
						it is nasal.

H as in German *ach*. Pronounce (k) without closing the breath passage.